Working Papers

for use with

Financial Accounting

Fourth Edition

Robert Libby
Cornell University – Ithaca

Patricia A. Libby
Ithaca College

Daniel G. Short
Miami University – Oxford

 Irwin

Boston   Burr Ridge, IL   Dubuque, IA   Madison, WI   New York   San Francisco   St. Louis
Bangkok   Bogotá   Caracas   Kuala Lumpur   Lisbon   London   Madrid   Mexico City
Milan   Montreal   New Delhi   Santiago   Seoul   Singapore   Sydney   Taipei   Toronto

Working Papers Notes for use with
FINANCIAL ACCOUNTING
Robert Libby, Patricia A. Libby, Daniel G. Short

Published by McGraw-Hill/Irwin, an imprint of The McGraw-Hill Companies, Inc., 1221 Avenue of the
Americas, New York, NY 10020. Copyright © 1996, 1998, 2001, 2004 by The McGraw-Hill Companies, Inc.
All rights reserved.

1 2 3 4 5 6 7 8 9 0 CUS/CUS 0 9 8 7 6 5 4 3 2

ISBN 0-07-247366-5

www.mhhe.com

CONTENTS

P1–2.

Requirement 1

SUSAN'S LAWN SERVICE
Income Statement
For the Three Months Ended August 31, 2003

Revenues from services:		
Total revenues		
Expenses:		
Total expenses		
Net income		

Requirement 2

P1–3.

Transaction	Requirement 1 Income	Cash	Requirement 2—Explanation
_____	_____	_____	_____
_____	_____	_____	_____
_____	_____	_____	_____
_____	_____	_____	_____
_____	_____	_____	_____
_____	_____	_____	_____
_____	_____	_____	_____
_____	_____	_____	_____
_____	_____	_____	_____
_____	_____	_____	_____
_____	_____	_____	_____
_____	_____	_____	_____
_____	_____	_____	_____
_____	_____	_____	_____
_____	_____	_____	_____
_____	_____	_____	_____
_____	_____	_____	_____
_____	_____	_____	_____
_____	_____	_____	_____
_____	_____	_____	_____
_____	_____	_____	_____
_____	_____	_____	_____
_____	_____	_____	_____
_____	_____	_____	_____
_____	_____	_____	_____
_____	_____	_____	_____
_____	_____	_____	_____
_____	_____	_____	_____

P1–4.
Requirement 1

_____

_____

Requirement 2

_____

_____

Requirement 3

_____

_____

Company resources:

_____

_____

_____

_____

_____

_____

_____

_____

_____

_____

_____

_____

_____

_____

Company obligations:

_____

_____

_____

_____

_____

_____

_____

_____

_____

_____

_____

_____

_____

_____

_____

_____

_____

Requirement 4

_____

_____

_____

_____

_____

AP1–1.

Requirement 1

MCCLAREN CORPORATION
Income Statement
For Year Ended June 30, 2005

Requirement 2

MCCLAREN CORPORATION
Balance Sheet
At June 30, 2005

Assets:

Liabilities:

Stockholders' Equity:

AP1–2.

Requirement 1

ABEL ELECTRIC REPAIR COMPANY, INC.
Income Statement
For the Three Months Ended December 31, 2003

Revenues from services:

    Total revenues

Expenses:

Requirement 2

CP1–1.

1. _____

2. _____

3. _____

4. _____

5. _____

CP1–2.

1. _____

_____

_____

_____

2. _____

_____

_____

_____

3. _____

_____

_____

_____

4. _____

_____

_____

_____

5. _____

_____

_____

_____

6. _____

_____

_____

_____

7. _____

_____

_____

_____

8. _____

_____

_____

_____

_____

_____

_____

_____

_____

_____

_____

_____

_____

_____

_____

_____

_____

_____

CP1–3.

1.

2.

3.

CP1–4.

Requirement 1—Deficiencies _____

_____

_____

_____

_____

_____

_____

_____

_____

_____

_____

_____

_____

_____

_____

_____

_____

Requirement 2

PERFORMANCE CORPORATION
Income Statement
For the Year Ended December 31, 2003

Revenues:		
Total revenues		
Expenses:		
Cost of goods sold		
Selling expenses		
Total expenses		
Pretax income		

CP–4. *(continued)*

Requirement 2 (continued)

PERFORMANCE CORPORATION
Balance Sheet
At December 31, 2003

Assets:		
Cash		
Merchandise inventory		
Supplies inventory		
Total assets		
Liabilities:		
Accounts payable		
Total liabilities		
Stockholders' Equity:		
Contributed capital		
Total stockholders' equity		
Total liabilities and stockholders' equity		

CP1–5.
Requirement 1

_____
_____
_____
_____
_____
_____
_____
_____
_____
_____
_____
_____
_____
_____
_____
_____
_____
_____
_____
_____
_____
_____

Requirement 2

_____
_____
_____
_____
_____
_____
_____
_____
_____
_____
_____
_____
_____
_____
_____
_____
_____
_____
_____
_____
_____
_____

CP1-6.
Requirement 1

_____
_____
_____
_____
_____
_____
_____

Requirement 2

_____
_____
_____
_____
_____
_____
_____
_____
_____
_____
_____
_____
_____

CP1-7.
Requirement 1

_____
_____
_____
_____
_____
_____
_____
_____
_____
_____
_____
_____

Requirement 2

_____
_____
_____
_____
_____
_____
_____
_____

Name _____ Date _____ Course _____ Section_____

CP1–8.

_____
_____
_____
_____
_____
_____
_____
_____
_____
_____
_____
_____
_____
_____
_____
_____
_____
_____
_____
_____
_____
_____
_____
_____
_____
_____
_____
_____
_____
_____
_____
_____

CP1–9.

_____
_____
_____
_____
_____
_____
_____
_____
_____
_____
_____
_____
_____
_____
_____
_____
_____
_____

M2–1.

(1) _____ (2) _____ (3) _____ (4) _____ (5) _____

M2–2.

(1) _____ (2) _____ (3) _____ (4) _____ (5) _____

M2–3.

$$\text{Financial Leverage} = \frac{\text{Average Total Assets}}{\text{Average Stockholders' Equity}} = \underline{\hspace{3cm}} = \underline{\hspace{2cm}} = \underline{\hspace{2cm}}$$

_____
_____
_____
_____
_____
_____
_____
_____

M2–4.

(1) _____ (2) _____ (3) _____ (4) _____ (5) _____ (6) _____

M2–5.

(1) _____ (2) _____ (3) _____ (4) _____ (5) _____ (6) _____ (7) _____ (8) _____
(9) _____ (10) _____ (11) _____ (12) _____ (13) _____ (14) _____ (15) _____ (16) _____

(Nor Bal)Inc side = Deb
(Nor Bal)Inc side = Cred

M2–6.

16300
1000
1000

	Assets		=	Liabilities	3,000	+	Stockholders' Equity	9800
a.	Cash	+1,000		Notes Payable	+1,000			
b.	Cash	+3000					Common Stock	+3,000
c.	Equip	+500		Notes payable	+400			
	Cash	-100						
d.	Cash	-100					dividends	-100
e.	Cash	-200		N/Rec payable	+200			

M2–7.

	Debit	Credit
Assets	increase	dec
Liabilities	dec	inc
Stockholders' equity	dec	inc

M2–8.

	Increase	Decrease
Assets	debit	credit
Liabilities	credit	debit
Stockholders' equity	credit	debit

M2–9.

Date	Item	DR Debit	CR Credit
a. Cash		1000	
N/Pay			1000
b. Cash		3000	
Contributed Cap			3000
c. Equip		500	
Cash			100
N/Pay			400
d. Ret earn		100	
Cash			100
e. N/Rec		200	
Cash			200

Compound entries { (bracket at c.)

M2–10.

Cash	Notes Receivable	Equipment

Notes Payable	Contributed Capital	Retained Earnings

Name McDougal, Cassie   Date 1/31   Course 201   Section 002

M2–11.

NARDOZZI, INC.
Balance Sheet
at January 31, 2003

Assets								Liabilities						
								Notes payable						
								Stockholders' Equity						
								Contributed capital						
								Retained earnings						
								Total Stockholders' Equity						
								Total Liabilities &						
Total Assets								*Stockholders' Equity*						

M2–12.

(a) _____ (b) _____ (c) _____ (d) _____ (e) _____

E2–1.

(1) _____ (2) _____ (3) _____ (4) _____ (5) _____
(6) _____ (7) _____ (8) _____ (9) _____ (10) _____

E2–2.

Requirement 1

	Given	Received	
(a)			
(b)			
(c)			
(d)			
(e)			
(f)			
(g)			
(h)			
(i)			
(j)			
(k)			
(l)			
(m)			

Requirement 2

Requirement 3

E2–3.

Account	Balance Sheet Categorization	Debit or Credit Balance
1.		
2.		
3.		
4.		
5.		
6.		
7.		
8.		
9.		
10.		

E2–4.

Assets		=	Liabilities		+	Stockholders' Equity	
a.							
b.							
c.							
d.							
e.							

E2–5.

Requirement 1

	Assets		=	Liabilities		+	Stockholders' Equity	
a.								
b.								
c.								
d.								
e.								

Requirement 2

_____

_____

_____

_____

_____

E2–6.

a.		
b.		
c.		
d.		
e.		

E2–7.

Requirement 1

a.

b.

c.

d.

e.

Requirement 2

E2–8.

Requirement 1

Cash	Note Receivable	Equipment

Land	Note Payable	Contributed Capital

Requirement 2

Assets $_____ = Liabilities $_____ + Stockholders' Equity $_____

Requirement 3

_____

_____

_____

_____

_____

_____

_____

Name _____ Date _____ Course _____ Section _____

E2–9.
Requirement 1

Transaction	Brief Explanation
1	
2	
3	
4	
5	
6	

Requirement 2

FAITH'S FINE FURNITURE COMPANY
Balance Sheet
at January 7, 2003

Assets		Liabilities	
		Stockholders' Equity	
		Total Stockholders' Equity	
Total Assets		*Total Liabilities &* *Stockholders' Equity*	

E2–10.

Requirement 1

Transaction	Brief Explanation
1	
2	
3	
4	
5	
6	

Requirement 2

FAYE'S FASHIONS, INC.
Balance Sheet
at March 31, 2004

Assets		Liabilities	
		Stockholders' Equity	
		Total Stockholders' Equity	
		Total Liabilities &	
Total Assets		Stockholders' Equity	

E2–16.

Transaction	Brief Explanation
(a)	
(b)	
(c)	
(d)	

E2–17.

Requirement 1

	Increases with…	Decreases with…
_____	_____	_____
_____	_____	_____
_____	_____	_____

Requirement 2

Equipment	Note Receivable	Notes Payable

	Beginning balance	+	"+"	–	"–"	=	Ending balance
Equipment		+		–		=	
Note receivable		+		–		=	
Note payable		+		–		=	

E2–18.

Activity	Type of Activity	Effect on Cash
(a) Reduction of long-term debt		
(b) Sale of land		
(c) Issuance of common stock		
(d) Capital expenditures		
(e) Issuance of long-term debt		

E2–19.

HILTON HOTELS CORPORATION
Partial Statement of Cash Flows
For the Year Ended December 31, 2003

Investing Activities

Financing Activities

E2–20.

1. Current assets	
2. Debt principal repaid	
3. Significant accounting policies	
4. Cash received on sale of noncurrent assets	
5. Dividends paid	
6. Short-term obligations	
7. Date of the statement of financial position	

P2–1.

Account	Balance Sheet Categorization	Debit or Credit Balance
(1)		
(2)		
(3)		
(4)		
(5)		
(6)		
(7)		
(8)		
(9)		
(10)		
(11)		
(12)		
(13)		
(14)		
(15)		

P2–2.

Requirement 1
_____
_____
_____
_____
_____
_____

Requirement 2 **(see next page)**

Requirement 3
_____
_____
_____
_____
_____

Requirement 4

(a) Total assets = _____

(b) Total liabilities = _____

(c) Total stockholders' equity = _____

(d) Cash balance = _____

(e) Total current assets = _____

P2–2. (continued)

Requirement 2

	Assets						=	Liabilities	+	Stockholders' Equity	
	Cash	Short-term Investments	Notes Receivable	Land	Building	Equipment		Notes Payable		Contributed Capital	Retained Earnings
(a)											
(b)											
(c)											
(d)											
(e)											
(f)											

P2–3.

Requirements 1 and 2

Cash	Short-Term Investments	Accounts Receivable

	Inventory	Long-Term Note Receivable

Equipment	Factory Building	Intangibles

Accounts Payable	Accrued Liabilities Payable	Short-Term Note Payable

Long-Term Note Payable	Contributed Capital	Retained Earnings

                                            Chapter 2

P2–3. (continued)
Requirement 3

_____
_____
_____
_____
_____
_____

Requirement 4

PATRIE PLASTICS COMPANY
Balance Sheet
at December 31, 2004

Assets		Liabilities	
		Stockholders' Equity	
		Total Liabilities &	
Total Assets		Stockholders' Equity	

Requirement 5

Financial Leverage $= \dfrac{\text{Average Total Assets}}{\text{Average Stockholders' Equity}} = \underline{\hspace{2cm}} = \underline{\hspace{2cm}} = \underline{\hspace{1cm}}$

_____
_____
_____
_____
_____
_____
_____

P2–4.

Transaction	Type of Activity	Effect on Cash
(a)		
(b)		
(c)		
(d)		
(e)		
(f)		
(g)		
(h)		
(i)		

P2–5.

Requirement 1

a.

b.

c.

d.

e.

f.

g.

h.

P2–5. (continued)

Requirement 2

Cash		Receivables & Other Assets		Inventories	

		Investments		Property, Plant & Equip.	

Intangible Assets		Accounts Payable		Other Short-Term Obligations	

Long-Term Liabilities		Contributed Capital		Retained Earnings	

44

P2–5. (continued)

Requirement 3

BAYER CORPORATION
Balance Sheet at December 31, 2001
(in millions of Euros)

ASSETS

LIABILITIES

STOCKHOLDERS' EQUITY

Requirement 4

$$\text{Financial Leverage} = \frac{\text{Average Total Assets}}{\text{Average Stockholders' Equity}} = \underline{\hspace{2cm}} = \underline{\hspace{2cm}} = \underline{\hspace{1cm}}$$

P2–6.

BAYER CORPORATION
Partial Statement of Cash Flows
For the Year Ended December 31, 2001
(in millions of Euros)

INVESTING ACTIVITIES							
FINANCING ACTIVITIES							

AP2–1.

Account	Balance Sheet Categorization	Debit or Credit Balance
(1)		
(2)		
(3)		
(4)		
(5)		
(6)		
(7)		
(8)		
(9)		
(10)		
(11)		
(12)		
(13)		
(14)		

AP2–2.
Requirement 1

	Assets					=	Liabilities		+	Stockholders' Equity	
	Cash	Notes Receivable	Long-Term Investments	Equipment	Building		Short-Term Notes Payable	Long-Term Notes Payable		Contributed Capital	Retained Earnings
(a)											
(b)											
(c)											
(d)											
(e)											
(f)											
(g)											
(h)											
(i)											

AP2–2. (continued)

Requirement 2

_____

_____
_____
_____
_____
_____
_____
_____

Requirement 3

(a)	
(b)	
(c)	

Name _____ Date _____ Course _____ Section _____

AP2–3.

Requirements 1 and 2

Cash and Cash
Equivalents

Short-Term Investments

Accounts Receivable

Inventories

Prepaid Expenses and
Other Current Assets

Property, Plant
and Equipment

Intangibles

Other Assets

Accounts Payable

Accrued Expenses Payable

Long-Term Debt

Other
Long-Term Liabilities

Contributed Capital

Retained Earnings

AP2–3. (continued)

Requirement 3

ETHAN ALLEN, INC.
Balance Sheet
at September 30, 2000
(in thousands of dollars)

Assets												
Total Assets												
Liabilities												
Total Liabilities												
Stockholders' Equity												
Total Stockholders' Equity												
Total Liabilities and Stockholders' Equity												

Requirement 4

$$\text{Financial Leverage} = \frac{\text{Average Total Assets}}{\text{Average Stockholders' Equity}} = \frac{}{} = \frac{}{} = \frac{}{}$$

AP2–4.

Transaction	Type of Activity	Effect on Cash
(a)		
(b)		
(c)		
(d)		
(e)		
(f)		
(g)		

CP2–1.

1. _____
_____
_____
_____

2. _____
_____
_____
_____
_____
_____
_____

3. _____
_____
_____
_____
_____

4. _____
_____
_____
_____
_____

5. _____
_____
_____
_____
_____

6.

$$\text{Financial Leverage} = \frac{\text{Average Total Assets}}{\text{Average Stockholders' Equity}} = \underline{\qquad} = \underline{\qquad} = \underline{\qquad}$$

_____
_____
_____

7. _____
_____
_____
_____
_____
_____

CP2–2.

1. _____

_____

_____

_____

_____

2. _____

_____

_____

_____

3. _____

_____

_____

_____

4.

$$\text{Financial Leverage} = \frac{\text{Average Total Assets}}{\text{Average Stockholders' Equity}} = \underline{\hspace{3cm}} = \underline{\hspace{2cm}} = \underline{\hspace{2cm}}$$

5. _____

_____

_____

_____

CP2–3.

1. _____

_____

_____

_____

2. _____

Current year		Abercrombie & Fitch	American Eagle Outfitters
Financial Leverage =	$\dfrac{\text{Average Total Assets}}{\text{Average Stockholders' Equity}}$	_____ = _____ =	_____ = _____ =

_____

_____

_____

_____

3. _____

	Industry Average	Abercrombie & Fitch	American Eagle Outfitters
Financial leverage =			

_____

_____

_____

_____

_____

_____

_____

_____

_____

_____

4. _____

_____

_____

_____

5. _____

_____

_____

_____

6. _____

_____

_____

_____

CP2-4.

1. (a) _____

   (b) _____
   _____
   _____
   _____

   (c) Financial Leverage $= \dfrac{\text{Average Total Assets}}{\text{Average Stockholders' Equity}} =$ _____ $=$ _____ $=$ _____

   _____
   _____
   _____
   _____
   _____
   _____
   _____

2. (a) _____
   _____

   (b) _____
   _____

CP2-5.

1. _____
_____

2. _____
_____
_____
_____
_____

3. _____
_____
_____
_____
_____
_____
_____
_____
_____

CP2-6.

_____
_____
_____
_____
_____
_____
_____
_____
_____
_____
_____
_____

CP2-7.

1. _____
_____

2. _____
_____
_____
_____

3. $\text{Financial Leverage} = \dfrac{\text{Average Total Assets}}{\text{Average Stockholders' Equity}} = \underline{\hspace{3cm}} = \underline{\hspace{2cm}} = \underline{\hspace{2cm}}$

_____
_____
_____
_____
_____
_____

4. _____
_____
_____
_____

5. _____
_____
_____
_____
_____

Retained earnings

CP2–8.

Requirement 1

McDONALD'S CORPORATION
Balance Sheets
at December 31
(in millions of dollars)

Assets	2003	2002
Total current assets		
Total Assets		
Liabilities		
Total current liabilities		
Total Liabilities		
Stockholders' Equity		
Total Stockholders' Equity		
Total Liabilities and Stockholders' Equity		

CP2–8. (continued)

Requirement 2

$$\text{Financial Leverage} = \frac{\text{Average Total Assets}}{\text{Average Stockholders' Equity}} = \underline{\hspace{4cm}} = \underline{\hspace{2cm}} = \underline{\hspace{2cm}}$$

Requirement 3

_____
_____
_____
_____
_____
_____

CP2–9.

Requirement 1

DEWEY, CHEETUM & HOWE, INC.
Balance Sheet
at December 31, 2004

Assets						
Total assets						
Liabilities						
Total current liabilities						
Total liabilities						
Stockholders' equity						
Total stockholders' equity						
Total liabilities and stockholders' equity						

CP2–9. (continued)

Requirement 2

Dear _____ ,

_____

_____

_____

_____

_____

_____

_____

_____

_____

_____

_____

_____

_____

_____

_____

_____

_____

_____

_____

CP2–10.

1. _____

_____

_____

_____

_____

_____

_____

_____

_____

_____

_____

_____

_____

_____

_____

_____

_____

_____

_____

CP2–10. (continued)

2. _____

3. _____

CP2–11.

M3–1.

TERM

_____ (1) Losses
_____ (2) Matching principle
_____ (3) Revenues
_____ (4) Time period assumption
_____ (5) Operating cycle

M3–2.

		2004	2005
Asset Turnover	$=\dfrac{\text{Sales}}{\text{Average Total Assets}}$	_____ =	_____ =

_____
_____
_____
_____

M3–3.

Cash Basis Income Statement								Accrual Basis Income Statement							

M3–4.

	Revenue Account Affected	Amount of Revenue Earned in July
a.		
b.		
c.		
d.		

M3–5.

	Expense Account Affected	Amount of Expenses Incurred in July
e.		
f.		
g.		
h.		
i.		

M3–6.

a.		
b.		
c.		
d.		

M3–7.

e.			
f.			
g.			
h.			
i.			

M3–8.

	Balance Sheet			Income Statement		
	Asset	Liabilities	Stockholders' Equity	Revenues	Expenses	Net Income
a.						
b.						
c.						
d.						

M3–9.

	Balance Sheet			Income Statement		
	Asset	Liabilities	Stockholders' Equity	Revenues	Expenses	Net Income
e.						
f.						
g.						
h.						
i.						

M3–10.

BOB'S BOWLING, INC.
Income Statement
For the Month of July 2004

M3–11.

BOB'S BOWLING, INC.
Partial Statement of Cash Flows
For the Month ended of July 31, 2004

E3–1.

TERM

_____ (1) Expenses
_____ (2) Gains
_____ (3) Revenue principle
_____ (4) Cash basis accounting
_____ (5) Unearned revenue
_____ (6) Operating cycle
_____ (7) Accrual basis accounting
_____ (8) Prepaid expenses
_____ (9) Revenues – Expenses = Net income
_____ (10) Ending Retained Earnings =
　　　　Beginning Retained Earnings + Net Income – Dividends

E3–2.

Activity	Revenue Account Affected	Amount of Revenue Earned in September
a.		
b.		
c.		
d.		
e.		
f.		
g.		
h.		
i.		
j.		
k.		
l.		
m.		

E3–3.

Activity	Expense Account Affected	Amount of Expense Incurred in January
a.		
b.		
c.		
d.		
e.		
f.		
g.		
h.		
i.		
j.		
k.		
l.		
m.		
n.		
o.		
p.		
q.		

E3–7.

Requirement 1

a.

b.

c.

d.

e.

f.

E3–7. (continued)

Requirement 1 (continued)

g. (1)

(2)

h.

i.

j.

k.

E3–13.

Requirement 1

THE TRAVELING GOURMET, INC.
Income Statement (unadjusted)
For the Month Ended March 31, 2005

Revenues:

Costs and expenses:

Net Income

Requirement 2

THE TRAVELING GOURMET, INC.
Statement of Retained Earnings (unadjusted)
For the Month Ended March 31, 2005

E3–13. (continued)

Requirement 3

THE TRAVELING GOURMET, INC.
Balance Sheet (unadjusted)
At March 31, 2005

Assets:

Liabilities:

Stockholders' Equity:

Requirement 4

E3–17.

Requirement 1

_____
_____
_____
_____
_____
_____
_____
_____
_____
_____
_____
_____
_____
_____
_____
_____

Requirement 2

Accounts Receivable	Prepaid Expenses	Unearned Revenue

Computations:

	Beginning balance	+	"+"	−	"−"	=	Ending balance
Accounts receivable		+		−		=	
Prepaid expenses		+		−		=	
Unearned revenues		+		−		=	

E3–18.

ITEM	LOCATION
1.	
2.	
3.	
4.	
5.	
6.	
7.	

Name _____ Date _____ Course _____ Section_____

P3–4.
Requirements 1 and 2

Cash		Accounts Receivable		Supplies	

Merchandise Inventory		Prepaid Expenses		Equipment	

Furniture and Fixtures		Accounts Payable		Notes Payable	

Contributed Capital		Sales Revenue		Cost of Goods Sold	

Advertising Expense		Wages Expense		Repair Expense	

P3–4. (continued)

Requirement 3

JENNA'S SWEETS
Income Statement (unadjusted)
For the Month Ended February 28, 2003

Revenues:							
Costs and expenses:							
Net Income							

JENNA'S SWEETS
Statement of Retained Earnings (unadjusted)
For the Month Ended February 28, 2003

P3–4. (continued)

JENNA'S SWEETS
Balance Sheet (unadjusted)
At February 28, 2003

Assets:

Liabilities:

Stockholders' Equity:

P3–4. (continued)

Requirement 4

_____
_____
_____
_____
_____
_____
_____
_____
_____
_____
_____
_____
_____
_____
_____
_____
_____
_____
_____
_____
_____
_____
_____
_____
_____
_____
_____
_____
_____
_____
_____
_____
_____
_____

Requirement 5

		2004	2005
Asset Turnover $=$	$\dfrac{\text{Sales}}{\text{Average Total Assets}}$	_____ $=$	_____ $=$

_____
_____
_____
_____
_____
_____

P3–5.

JENNA'S SWEETS
Statement of Cash Flows
For the Month Ended February 28, 2003

Operating Activities

Investing Activities

Financing Activities

Increase in cash

Ending cash balance

P3–6.

Requirements 1 and 2

ASSETS:

Cash	Receivables	Flight and Ground Equipment

Prepaid Expenses	Other Assets	Spare Parts, Supplies, and Fuel

LIABILITIES:

Accounts Payable	Accrued Expenses Payable	Long-Term Notes Payable

STOCKHOLDERS' EQUITY:

Other Noncurrent Liabilities	Contributed Capital	Retained Earnings

REVENUES AND EXPENSES:

Delivery Service Revenue	Rental Expense	Repair Expense

Wage Expense	Fuel Expense

P3–6. (continued)

Requirement 3

FEDERAL EXPRESS CORPORATION
Income Statement (unadjusted)
For the Month Ended June 30, 2004
(in millions)

Revenues:		
Costs and expenses:		
Net Income		

FEDERAL EXPRESS CORPORATION
Statement of Retained Earnings (unadjusted)
For the Month Ended June 30, 2004
(in millions)

Retained earnings, May 31, 2004		
Retained earnings, June 30, 2004		

P3–6. (continued)

FEDERAL EXPRESS CORPORATION
Balance Sheet (unadjusted)
At June 30, 2004
(in millions)

Assets								
Total Assets								
Liabilities								
Total Liabilities								
Stockholders' Equity								
Total stockholders' equity								
Total liabilities and stockholders' equity								

P3–6. (continued)

FEDERAL EXPRESS CORPORATION
Statement of Cash Flows
For the Month Ended June 30, 2004
(in millions)

Operating Activities

Investing Activities

Financing Activities

Increase in cash

Ending cash balance

Requirement 4

Asset Turnover = $\dfrac{\text{Sales}}{\text{Average Total Assets}}$ = _____ = _____

P3–7.

Requirement 1

	a.		
b.			
c.			
d.			
e.			
f.			
g.			
h.			
i.			
j.			
k.			
l.			

P3–7. (continued)

Requirement 2

Transaction	Operating, Investing, or Financing Effect	Direction and Amount of the Effect
(a)		
(b)		
(c)		
(d)		
(e)		
(f)		
(g)		
(h)		
(i)		
(j)		
(k)		
(l)		

AP3–1.

Transaction	Debit	Credit
a.		
b.		
c.		
d.		
e.		
f.		
g.		
h.		
i.		
j.		
k.		
l.		
m.		
n.		
o.		
p.		

AP3–2.

AP3–3.

Requirement 1   *Requirement 2*

	Balance Sheet			Income Statement			Statement of Cash Flows
	Assets	Liabilities	Stockholders' Equity	Revenues	Expenses	Net Income	
a.							
b.							
c.							
d.							
e.							
f.							
g.							
h.							
i.							
j.							
k.							

AP3–4.

Requirements 1 & 2

Cash

Accounts Receivable

Supplies

Barns

Land

Prepaid Insurance

Accounts Payable

Unearned Revenue

Long-Term Note Payable

AP3–4. (continued)
Requirements 1 & 2 (continued)

Contributed Capital	Retained Earnings

Animal Care Service Revenue	Rental Revenue

Utilities Expense	Wages Expense

Requirement 3

SPICEWOOD STABLES, INC.
Income Statement (unadjusted)
For the Month Ended April 30, 2003

Revenues:		
Costs and expenses		
Net Income		

SPICEWOOD STABLES, INC.
Statement of Retained Earnings (unadjusted)
For the Month Ended April 30, 2003

AP3–4. (continued)

SPICEWOOD STABLES, INC.
Balance Sheet (unadjusted)
At April 30, 2003

Assets:		
Total assets		
Liabilities:		
Total Liabilities		
Stockholders' Equity:		
Total stockholders' equity		
Total liabilities and stockholders' equity		

Requirement 4

AP3–4. (continued)
Requirement 5

2004: $\dfrac{\text{Asset}}{\text{Turnover}} = \dfrac{\text{Sales}}{\begin{array}{c}\text{Average}\\\text{Total Assets}\end{array}} = \underline{\hspace{3cm}} = \underline{\hspace{2cm}} =$

2005: $\dfrac{\text{Asset}}{\text{Turnover}} = \dfrac{\text{Sales}}{\begin{array}{c}\text{Average}\\\text{Total Assets}\end{array}} = \underline{\hspace{3cm}} = \underline{\hspace{2cm}} =$

AP3–5.

SPICEWOOD STABLES, INC.
Statement of Cash Flows
For the Month Ended April 30, 2003

Operating Activities	
Investing Activities	
Financing Activities	
Increase in cash	
Ending cash balance	

AP3–6.

Requirements 1 and 2 (in millions)

ASSETS:

Cash	Marketable Securities	Accounts Receivable

Inventories	Prepaid Expenses	Investments

Property & Equipment	Intangibles (net)

LIABILITIES:

Accounts Payable	Notes Payable	Income Tax Payable

Other Debt	**SHAREHOLDERS' EQUITY:**
	Shareholders' Equity

REVENUES AND EXPENSES:

Sales Revenue	Cost of Sales	Wages Expense

Utilities Expense	Interest Expense

AP3–6. (continued)

Requirement 3

EXXON CORPORATION
Income Statement (unadjusted)
For the Month Ended January 31, 2005
(in millions)

Revenues:

Costs and expenses:

Net Income

EXXON CORPORATION
Statement of Retained Earnings (unadjusted)
For the Month Ended January 31, 2005
(in millions)

AP3–6. (continued)

EXXON CORPORATION
Balance Sheet (unadjusted)
At January 31, 2005
(in millions)

Assets

Total Assets

Liabilities

Total Liabilities

Shareholders' Equity

Total liabilities and shareholders' equity

AP3–6. (continued)

EXXON CORPORATION
Statement of Cash Flows
For the Month Ended January 31, 2005
(in millions)

Operating Activities						
Investing Activities						
Financing Activities						
Increase in cash						
Ending cash balance						

Requirement 4

$$\text{Asset Turnover} = \frac{\text{Sales}}{\text{Average Total Assets}} = \underline{\hspace{2cm}} = \underline{\hspace{2cm}}$$

CP3–1.

1. _____
_____
_____
_____
_____
_____
_____

2. _____
_____
_____
_____

3. _____
_____
_____

Accounts Receivable

4. _____
_____
_____
_____
_____
_____
_____
_____
_____
_____

5. _____
_____
_____
_____
_____
_____
_____

6.

$$\text{Asset Turnover} = \frac{\text{Sales}}{\text{Average Total Assets}} = \underline{\quad} = \underline{\quad} = \underline{\quad}$$

_____
_____
_____

CP3–2.

1. _____

_____

_____

_____

_____

_____

_____

2. _____

_____

_____

Inventory

3. _____

_____

_____

_____

_____

_____

_____

_____

_____

_____

4.

$$\text{Asset Turnover} = \frac{\text{Sales}}{\text{Average Total Assets}} = \underline{\quad} = \underline{\quad} = \underline{\quad}$$

_____

_____

_____

_____

CP3–2.

1. _____
_____
_____
_____
_____
_____
_____
_____

2. _____
_____
_____
_____
_____
_____
_____
_____

3. _____
_____
_____
_____
_____
_____
_____
_____

4.

$$\text{Asset Turnover} = \frac{\text{Sales}}{\text{Average Total Assets}}$$

American Eagle Outfitters	Abercrombie & Fitch
_____ =	_____ =

_____
_____
_____
_____

5.

	Industry Average	American Eagle Outfitters	Abercrombie & Fitch
Asset Turnover =			

_____
_____
_____
_____

CP3–3. (continued)

6. _____

_____

_____

_____

_____

7. _____

_____

_____

CP3–4.

Requirement 1

1998:   Asset Turnover $= \dfrac{\text{Sales}}{\text{Average Total Assets}} =$ _____ $=$ _____ $=$

1999:   Asset Turnover $= \dfrac{\text{Sales}}{\text{Average Total Assets}} =$ _____ $=$ _____ $=$

2000:   Asset Turnover $= \dfrac{\text{Sales}}{\text{Average Total Assets}} =$ _____ $=$ _____ $=$

2001:   Asset Turnover $= \dfrac{\text{Sales}}{\text{Average Total Assets}} =$ _____ $=$ _____ $=$

Requirement 2

1998:   Financial Leverage $= \dfrac{\text{Average Total Assets}}{\text{Average Stockholders' Equity}} =$ _____ $=$ _____ $=$

1999:   Financial Leverage $= \dfrac{\text{Average Total Assets}}{\text{Average Stockholders' Equity}} =$ _____ $=$ _____ $=$

2000:   Financial Leverage $= \dfrac{\text{Average Total Assets}}{\text{Average Stockholders' Equity}} =$ _____ $=$ _____ $=$

2001:   Financial Leverage $= \dfrac{\text{Average Total Assets}}{\text{Average Stockholders' Equity}} =$ _____ $=$ _____ $=$

Requirement 3 _____

_____

_____

_____

_____

_____

CP3–5.
Requirement 1

_____
_____
_____
_____
_____
_____
_____

Requirement 2

_____
_____
_____
_____
_____
_____
_____

Requirement 3

_____
_____
_____
_____
_____
_____
_____
_____
_____
_____
_____
_____
_____
_____
_____
_____

CP3–6.

Requirement 1

a. and b. _____

_____

c. _____

_____

_____

_____

d. _____

_____

_____

_____

e. _____

_____

_____

_____

f. _____

_____

_____

_____

g. _____

_____

_____

_____

h. _____

_____

_____

_____

i. _____

_____

_____

_____

j. _____

_____

_____

_____

CP3–6. (continued)
Requirement 2

TASTLE PAINTING SERVICE COMPANY
Income Statement (unadjusted)
For the Month Ended January 31, 2004

Revenues:

Costs and expenses:

Net Income

TASTLE PAINTING SERVICE COMPANY
Statement of Retained Earnings (unadjusted)
For the Month Ended January 31, 2004

CP3–6. (continued)

Requirement 2 (continued)

TASTLE PAINTING SERVICE COMPANY
Balance Sheet (unadjusted)
At January 31, 2004

Assets:	
Total assets	
Liabilities:	
Total Liabilities	
Shareholders' Equity:	
Total shareholders' equity	
Total liabilities and shareholders' equity	

Requirement 3

Transaction	Operating, Investing, or Financing Effect	Direction and Amount of the Effect
(a)		
(b)		
(c)		
(d)		
(e)		
(f)		
(g)		
(h)		
(i)		
(j)		

Name _____ Date _____ Course _____ Section_____

CP3–7.

CP3–8.

Requirement 1

Requirement 2

CP3-8. (continued)
Requirement 2 (continued)
ASSETS:

Cash	Accounts Receivable	Supplies

Building	Land	Tools and Equipment

LIABILITIES:

Accounts Payable	Unearned Revenue

SHAREHOLDERS' EQUITY:

Contributed Capital	Retained Earnings

REVENUES AND EXPENSES:

Service Fee Revenue	Operating Expenses	Supplies Expense

Loss from Theft

CP3-8. (continued)
Requirement 3

TELLO COMPANY
Income Statement (unadjusted)
For the Year Ended December 31, 2004

Revenues:				
Costs and expenses:				
Net Income				

a.

b.

c.

d.

e.

f.

g.

h.

i.

j.

k.

CP3–8. (continued)

Requirement 3 (continued)

TELLO COMPANY
Balance Sheet (unadjusted)
At December 31, 2004

Assets		
Total Assets		
Liabilities		
Total current liabilities		
Shareholders' Equity		
Total shareholders' equity		
Total liabilities and shareholders' equity		

TELLO COMPANY
Statement of Cash Flows
For the Year Ended December 31, 2004

Operating Activities		
Investing Activities		
Financing Activities		
Increase in cash		
Ending cash balance		

CP3–8. (continued)

Requirement 4

CP3–8. (continued)

Requirement 5

CP3–9.

CP3–10.

M4–11.

Revenues:	
Costs and expenses:	
Net Income	

M4–12.

E4–1.

GOODISON CONSULTANTS, INC.
Unadjusted Trial Balance
At September 30, 2004

	Debit	Credit
Cash		
Accounts receivable		
Supplies inventory		
Prepaid expenses		
Investments		
Building and equipment		
Accumulated depreciation		
Land		
Accounts payable		
Accrued expenses payable		
Unearned consulting fees		
Income taxes payable		
Notes payable		
Contributed capital		
Retained earnings		
Consulting fees earned		
Investment income		
Wages and benefits expense		
Utilities expense		
Travel expense		
Rent expense		
Professional development expense		
Interest expense		
Other operating expenses		
General and administrative expense		
Gain on sale of land		
Totals		

E4–2.

Requirement 1

Balance sheet account	Related Income statement account

Requirement 2

Balance sheet account	Related Income statement account

E4–3.

Requirement 1

_____

_____

_____

Requirement 2

Adjusting journal entry:

(a) Date: _____

_____

Explanation: _____

_____

_____

(b) Date: _____

_____

Explanation: _____

_____

Requirement 3

_____

_____

_____

_____

_____

_____

_____

E4–4.

Requirement 1

2004 Income Statement:

    Insurance expense: _____

    Shipping supplies expense: _____

Requirement 2

2004 Balance sheet:

    Prepaid insurance: _____

    Shipping supplies inventory: _____

Requirement 3

	Prepaid Insurance			Insurance Expense	

Requirement 4

	Shipping Supplies Inventory			Shipping Supplies Expense	

E4-5.

	Balance Sheet			Income Statement		
	Assets	Liabilities	Stockholders' Equity	Revenues	Expenses	Net Income
E4-3(a)						
E4-3(b)						
E4-4(a)						
E4-4(b)						

E4–6.

Requirements 1 and 2

a.

b.

c.

d.

e.

f.

g.

Name _____ Date _____ Course _____ Section _____

E4–7.

	Balance Sheet			Income Statement		
	Assets	Liabilities	Stockholders' Equity	Revenues	Expenses	Net Income
(a)						
(b)						
(c)						
(d)						
(e)						
(f)						
(g)						

E4–8.

	Debit		Credit	
	Code	Amount	Code	Amount
a.				
b.				
c.				
d.				
e.				
f.				
g.				
h.				
i.				

E4–9.

Selected Balance Sheet Amounts at December 31, 2004:

Assets:

Selected Income Statement Amounts for the Year Ended December 31, 2004:

E4–10.

Date	Balance Sheet			Income Statement		
	Assets	Liabilities	Stockholders' Equity	Revenues	Expenses	Net Income
April 1, 2003 Receipt of Note 1						
December 31, 2003 Adjustment for Note 1						
March 31, 2004 Collection of Note 1						
August 1, 2003 Borrowing on Note 2						
December 31, 2003 Adjustment for Note 2						
July 31, 2004 Payment on Note 2						

E4–11.

Requirement 1

(a) _____

(b) _____

(c) _____

(d) _____

(e) _____

(f) _____

Requirement 2   Computations:

(a)

Beg. Bal.	+	accrued income taxes	–	cash paid	=	End Bal.
	+		–		=	
	+		–		=	
	+				=	

(c)

Beg. Bal.	+	dividends declared	–	cash paid	=	End Bal.
	+		–		=	
	+		–		=	
	+				=	

(f)

Beg. Bal.	+	accrued interest expense	–	cash paid	=	End Bal.
	+		–		=	
	+		–		=	
	+		–		=	

E4–12.

Requirement 1

Adjusting entries that were or should have been made at December 31:

a.

b.

c.

d.

e.

Requirement 2

	Balance Sheet			Income Statement		
	Assets	Liabilities	Stockholders' Equity	Revenues	Expenses	Net Income
(a)						
(b)						
(c)						
(d)						
(e)						

E4–13.

Items	Net Income	Total Assets	Total Liabilities	Stockholders' Equity
Balances reported				
Effects of:				
a. Depreciation				
b. Wages				
c. Rent revenue				
Adjusted balances				
d. Effects of income taxes				
Correct balances				

Computations:

(a) _____

(b) _____

(c) _____

_____

(d) _____

_____

P4–1.

DELL COMPUTER CORPORATION
Adjusted Trial Balance
At January 29, 2003

	Debit	Credit

P4-2.

Requirement 1

a.		e.	
b.		f.	
c.		g.	
d.		h.	

Requirement 2

a.

b.

c.

d.

e.

f.

g.

h.

P4–3.

Requirement 1

a.		e.	
b.		f.	
c.		g.	
d.		h.	

Requirement 2

	Balance Sheet			Income Statement		
	Assets	Liabilities	Stockholders' Equity	Revenues	Expenses	Net Income
a.						
b.						
c.						
d.						
e.						
f.						
g.						
h.						

P4–4.

Requirement 1

a.		e.	
b.		f.	
c.		g.	
d.		h.	

Requirement 2

a.

b.

P4–4. (continued)

c.

d.

e.

f.

g.

h.

P4–5.

Requirement 1

a.		e.	
b.		f.	
c.		g.	
d.		h.	

Requirement 2

	Balance Sheet			Income Statement		
	Assets	Liabilities	Stockholders' Equity	Revenues	Expenses	Net Income
a.						
b.						
c.						
d.						
e.						
f.						
g.						
h.						

Computations:

a.

b.

c.

d.

e.

f.

g.

h.

P4–6.

Rent Revenue			Salary Expenses			Maintenance Supplies Expense	

Rent Receivable			Receivables from Employees			Maintenance Supplies Inventory	

Unearned Rent Revenue			Salaries Payable	

Cash	

Item	Description	Location
1.		
2.		
3.		
4.		
5.		
6.		
7.		
8.		
9.		
10.		
11.		

P4–7.

Requirement 1

December 31, 2003 Adjusting Entries		Ref.
(1)		
(2)		
(3)		
(4)		

Requirement 2

	Amounts before Adjusting Entries	Amounts after Adjusting Entries
Revenues:		
Expenses:		
Net income (loss)		

Requirement 3

Earnings per share = _____

P4–7. (continued)
Requirement 4

Net profit margin = _____

_____

_____

_____

_____

_____

Requirement 5

P4–8.
Requirement 1

December 31, 2004 Adjusting Entries:

a.

b.

c.

d.

e.

P4–8. (continued)

Requirement 2

DORN, INC.
Income Statement
For the Year Ended December 31, 2004

Revenues:	
Expenses:	
Net Income	
Earnings per share	

DORN, INC.
Balance Sheet
At December 31, 2004

Assets		*Liabilities*	
		Stockholders' Equity	
Total assets		**Total liabilities and stockholders' equity**	

Requirement 3   **December 31, 2004 Closing Entries:**

a.	
b.	

P4–9.

Requirements 1, 2, 3, 5, and 6 T-accounts

Cash	Accounts Receivable	Supplies

Land	Equipment	Accumulated Depreciation

Remaining Assets	Accounts Payable	Notes Payable

Wages Payable	Interest Payable	Income Taxes Payable

Contributed Capital	Retained Earnings	Service Revenue

Depreciation Expense	Income Tax Expense	Interest Expense

Remaining Expenses

P4–9. (continued)
Requirement 2

(a)

(b)

(c)

(d)

(e)

(f)

(g)

(h)

(i)

(j)

(k)

P4–9. (continued)
Requirement 3

(l)

(m)

(n)

(o)

(p)

Requirement 4

H & H TOOL, INC.
Income Statement
For the Year Ended December 31, 2003
(in thousands)

Revenues:								
Expenses:								
Net income								
Earnings per share								

P4–9. (continued)

Requirement 4 (continued)

H & H TOOL, INC.
Statement of Stockholders' Equity
For the Year Ended December 31, 2003
(in thousands)

	Contributed Capital	Retained Earnings	Total Stockholders' Equity
Balance, January 1, 2003			
Balance, December 31, 2003			

H & H TOOL, INC.
Balance Sheet
At December 31, 2003
(in thousands)

Assets:		Liabilities:	
		Stockholders' Equity:	
Total assets		**Total Liabilities and stockholders' equity**	

P4–9. (continued)

Requirement 4 (concluded)

H & H TOOL, INC.
Statement of Cash Flows
For the Period Ended December 31, 2003
(in thousands)

Cash from Operating Activities:														
Cash from Investing Activities:														
Cash from Financing Activities:														
Change in cash														
Beginning cash balance, January 1, 2003														
Ending cash balance, December 31, 2003														

Requirement 5

Closing entries for December 31, 2003:

(1)														
(2)														

P4–9. (concluded)

Requirement 6

H & H TOOL, INC.
Post-Closing Trial Balance
At December 31, 2003
(in thousands)

Account	No.	Debit	Credit

Requirement 7

(a)   Financial leverage   = _____

(b)   Total asset turnover   = _____

(c)   Net profit margin   = _____

AP4–1.

STARBUCKS CORPORATION
Adjusted Trial Balance
At September 30, 2003

	Debit	Credit

AP4–2.

Requirement 1

a.		e.	
b.		f.	
c.		g.	
d.		h.	

Name _____ Date _____ Course _____ Section _____

AP4–2. (continued)
Requirement 2

a.

b.

c.

d.

e.

f.

g.

h.

AP4–3.

Requirement 1

a.		e.	
b.		f.	
c.		g.	
d.		h.	

Requirement 2

	Balance Sheet			Income Statement		
	Assets	Liabilities	Stockholders' Equity	Revenues	Expenses	Net Income
a.						
b.						
c.						
d.						
e.						
f.						
g.						
h.						

AP4–4.

Requirement 1

a.		e.	
b.		f.	
c.		g.	
d.		h.	

Requirement 2

a.

b.

162

AP4–4. (continued)

c.

d.

e.

f.

g.

h.

AP4–5.

Requirement 1

a.		e.	
b.		f.	
c.		g.	
d.		h.	

Requirement 2

	Balance Sheet			Income Statement		
	Assets	Liabilities	Stockholders' Equity	Revenues	Expenses	Net Income
a.						
b.						
c.						
d.						
e.						
f.						
g.						
h.						

Computations:

a.

b.

c.

d.

e.

f.

g.

h.

Name _____ Date _____ Course _____ Section _____

AP4–6.

Service Revenue	Cleaning Supplies Expense	Accounts Receivable

Cleaning Supplies Inventory	Wages Expense	Unearned Revenue

Wages Payable	Cash

Item	Description	Location
1.		
2.		
3.		
4.		
5.		
6.		
7.		
8.		
9.		
10.		

AP4–7.

Requirement 1

December 31, 2003 Adjusting Entries: *Ref.*

(1)

(2)

(3)

(4)

(5)

Requirement 2

	Amounts before Adjusting Entries	Amounts after Adjusting Entries
Revenues:		
Expenses:		
Net income (loss)		

AP4–7. (continued)
Requirement 3

Earnings per share = _____

Requirement 4

Net profit margin = _____

_____

_____

Requirement 5

AP4–8.
Requirement 1

December 31, 2004 Adjusting Entries:

a.	
b.	
c.	
d.	
e.	

AP4–8. (continued)

Requirement 2

RHOADES CO.
Income Statement
For the Year Ended December 31, 2004

Revenues:	
Expenses:	
Net Income	
Earnings per share	

RHOADES CO.
Balance Sheet
At December 31, 2004

Assets		*Liabilities*	
		Stockholders' Equity	
Total assets		*Total liabilities and stockholders' equity*	

Requirement 3   **December 31, 2004 Closing Entries:**

a.	
b.	

AP4–9.

Requirements 1, 2, 3, 5, and 6 T-accounts

Cash	Accounts Receivable	Supplies Inventory

Small Tools Inventory	Equipment	Accumulated Depreciation

Remaining Assets	Accounts Payable	Notes Payable

Wages Payable	Interest Payable	Income Taxes Payable

Unearned Revenue	Contributed Capital	Retained Earnings

Service Revenue	Income Tax Expense	Interest Expense

Depreciation Expense	Remaining Expenses

AP4–9. (continued)

Requirement 2

(a)

(b)

(c)

(d)

(e)

(f)

(g)

(h)

(i)

(j)

(k)

AP4–9. (continued)

Requirement 3

(l)

(m)

(n)

(o)

(p)

Requirement 4

NEW AGAIN FURNITURE, INC.
Income Statement
For the Year Ended December 31, 2003
(in thousands)

Revenues:

Expenses:

Net income

Earnings per share

AP4–9. (continued)
Requirement 4 (continued)

NEW AGAIN FURNITURE, INC.
Statement of Stockholders' Equity
For the Year Ended December 31, 2003
(in thousands)

	Contributed Capital	Retained Earnings	Total Stockholders' Equity

NEW AGAIN FURNITURE, INC.
Balance Sheet
At December 31, 2003
(in thousands)

Assets:		Liabilities:	
		Stockholders' Equity:	
Total assets		Total Liabilities and stockholders' equity	

AP4–9. (continued)

Requirement 4 (concluded)

NEW AGAIN FURNITURE, INC.
Statement of Cash Flows
For the Period Ended December 31, 2003
(in thousands)

Cash from Operating Activities:		
Cash from Investing Activities:		
Cash from Financing Activities:		
Change in cash		
Beginning cash balance, January 1, 2003		
Ending cash balance, December 31, 2003		

Requirement 5

December 31, 2003 Closing Entries:

(1)		
(2)		

AP4–9. (concluded)

Requirement 6

NEW AGAIN FURNITURE, INC.
Post-Closing Trial Balance
At December 31, 2003
(in thousands)

Account	Account Titles	Debit	Credit
	Totals		

Requirement 7

(a) Financial leverage   =   _____

(b) Total asset turnover   =   _____

(c) Net profit margin   =   _____

Name _____ Date _____ Course _____ Section _____

CP4–1.

1. _____
   _____
   _____

2. _____
   _____
   _____
   _____
   _____

3. _____
   _____
   _____
   _____
   _____

4. _____
   _____
   _____
   _____

5. _____
   _____
   _____
   _____

6. _____
   _____
   _____

7. _____
   _____
   _____
   _____

8. _____
   _____
   _____

9.   1998: Net Profit Margin $= \dfrac{\text{Net Income}}{\text{Sales}} =$ _____ $=$

     1999: Net Profit Margin $= \dfrac{\text{Net Income}}{\text{Sales}} =$ _____ $=$

     2000: Net Profit Margin $= \dfrac{\text{Net Income}}{\text{Sales}} =$ _____ $=$

_____
_____
_____
_____
_____
_____
_____

CP4–2.

1. _____

_____

_____

_____

_____

2. _____

_____

_____

_____

_____

3. _____

_____

_____

_____

_____

4. _____

5. 1998: Net Profit Margin $= \dfrac{\text{Net Income}}{\text{Sales}} =$ _____ $=$

    1999: Net Profit Margin $= \dfrac{\text{Net Income}}{\text{Sales}} =$ _____ $=$

    2000: Net Profit Margin $= \dfrac{\text{Net Income}}{\text{Sales}} =$ _____ $=$

_____

_____

_____

_____

_____

_____

_____

Name _____ Date _____ Course _____ Section _____

CP4–3.

1.
_____
_____
_____
_____
_____
_____
_____
_____
_____
_____
_____

2.

Year		American Eagle Outfitters		Abercrombie & Fitch
2000				
1999				
1998				

_____
_____
_____
_____
_____

3.

	Industry Average	American Eagle Outfitters	Abercrombie & Fitch
Advertising/Sales =			

_____
_____
_____
_____
_____
_____
_____
_____
_____
_____
_____
_____

CP4–3. (concluded)

4.

_____
_____
_____
_____
_____
_____
_____

5.

		American Eagle Outfitters	Abercrombie & Fitch
1998:	Net Profit Margin $=$ $\dfrac{\text{Net Income}}{\text{Sales}}$	_____ $=$	_____ $=$
1999:	Net Profit Margin $=$ $\dfrac{\text{Net Income}}{\text{Sales}}$	_____ $=$	_____ $=$
2000:	Net Profit Margin $=$ $\dfrac{\text{Net Income}}{\text{Sales}}$	_____ $=$	_____ $=$

_____
_____
_____
_____
_____
_____
_____
_____
_____
_____
_____
_____

6.

	Industry Average	American Eagle Outfitters	Abercrombie & Fitch
Net Profit Margin $=$			

_____
_____
_____
_____
_____

CP4–4.

1. _____
_____
_____
_____
_____
_____

2. _____
_____
_____
_____
_____
_____

3. _____
_____
_____
_____
_____
_____
_____
_____
_____
_____

CP4–5.

Requirement 1

Account	Unadjusted Trial Balance		Adjusted Trial Balance		Post-Closing Trial Balance	
	Debit	Credit	Debit	Credit	Debit	Credit

CP4–5. (continued)
Requirement 2

(a) _____

_____

_____

(b) _____

_____

_____

(c) _____

_____

_____

(d) _____

_____

_____

(e) _____

_____

_____

(f) _____

_____

Requirement 3   **Closing Entries on December 31, 2003:**

(1)	
(2)	

Requirement 4

Pretax income X	Average income tax rate =	Income tax expense

Requirement 5

Number of shares issued   X   Average issue price   =   Total issue amount

_____ X _____ = _____

_____ = _____

CP4–6.

Transaction A:

1. _____

_____

_____

_____

_____

2. _____

_____

_____

_____

_____

_____

3. Balance sheet at December 31, 2004:

Assets:							

4. _____

_____

_____

_____

_____

_____

_____

_____

_____

_____

_____

CP4–6. (continued)
Transaction B:
1. _____

2. _____

3. _____

4. _____

Transaction C:
1. _____

2. _____

3. _____

CP4–6. (continued)
Transaction D:

1.

2.

3.

CP4–7.

Requirement 1

Adjusting entries:

(a)

(b)

(c)

(d)

(e)

(f)

Requirement 2

Closing entries (from the adjusted trial balance):

(1)

(2)

CP4–7. (continued)
Requirement 3

a. _____

b. _____

c. _____

d. _____

e. _____

f. _____

g. _____

h. _____

i. _____

j. _____

CP4–8.

Requirement 1

CRYSTAL'S DAY SPA
Income Statement
For the Year Ended December 31, 2003

Items	Cash Basis Per Crystal's Statement	Explanation of Changes	Corrected Basis

Requirement 2

1. _____
_____
_____
_____
_____
_____
_____
_____

CP4–8. (continued)

2. _____
a. _____
b. _____
c. _____
d. _____
e. _____
f. _____
g. _____

CP4–9.

Requirement 1

2003		Debit	Credit
12/31	**Adjusting Entries**		
(a)			
(b)			
(c)			
(d)			
(e)			
(f)			

CP4–9. (continued)
Requirement 2

MONROEVILLE MOVING CORPORATION
Corrections to 2003 Financial Statements

Item	Amounts Reported	Ref.	Changes		Corrected Amounts
			Plus	Minus	
2003 Income Statement:					
December 31, 2003 Balance Sheet					

CP4–9. (continued)
Requirement 3

Omission of adjusting entries caused:

(a) _____

(b) _____

Requirement 4

(a) Earnings per share:

   Unadjusted – _____

   Adjusted – _____

(b) Net profit margin:

   Unadjusted – _____

   Adjusted – _____

Requirement 5

_____
_____
_____
_____
_____
_____
_____
_____
_____
_____
_____
_____
_____
_____
_____
_____
_____
_____
_____
_____
_____
_____
_____
_____

CP4–9. (concluded)

CP4–10.

M5–1.

Players	Definitions
_____ (1) CEO and CFO	A. Adviser who analyzes financial and other economic information to form forecasts and stock recommendations.
_____ (2) Independent auditor	B. Institutional and private investors and creditors (among others)
_____ (3) Users	C. Chief Executive Officer and Chief Financial Officer who have primary responsibility for the information presented in financial statements.
_____ (4) Financial analyst	D. Independent CPA who examines financial statements and attests to their fairness.

M5–2.

No.	Title
_____	Annual report
_____	Form 10K
_____	Earnings press release

M5–3.

Elements of Financial Statements

Financial Statements

_____ (1) Liabilities

_____ (2) Cash from operating activities

_____ (3) Losses

_____ (4) Assets

_____ (5) Revenues

_____ (6) Cash from financial activities

_____ (7) Gains

_____ (8) Owners' equity

_____ (9) Expenses

_____ (10) Assets owned by stockholder

A. Income statement.
B. Balance sheet.
C. Cash flow statement.
D. None of the above.

M5–4.

	Transaction	Current Assets	Gross Profit	Current Liabilities
(a)				
(b)				

Journal Entries (optional)

(a)	

(b)	

M5–5.

Assets	Liabilities	Stockholders' Equity

E5–6.

Requirement 1

LANCE, INC.
Consolidated Balance Sheet
December 31, Current Year
(in millions)

ASSETS

LIABILITIES

STOCKHOLDERS' EQUITY

E5–6. (continued)
Requirement 2

_____
_____
_____
_____
_____
_____
_____
_____
_____

E5–7.

	2004	*2005*	*2006*	*2007*

E5–8.

Assets	*Liabilities*	*Stockholders' Equity*

E5–9.

E5–10.

E5–15.

Transaction	Current Assets	Gross Profit	Current Liabilities
(a)			
(b)			
(c)			

(a)

(b)

(c)

E5–16.

Transaction	Current Assets	Gross Profit	Current Liabilities	Cash Flow from Operating Activities
(a)				
(b)				

(a)

(b)

E5–17.

BLACKWELL CORPORATION
Statement of Cash Flows
For the Year Ended December 31, 2003

E5–18.

Requirement 1

	Current Year	Prior Year
Net income (given) ⎯⎯⎯⎯⎯⎯⎯⎯ Average Shareholders' Equity (given)		

_____

_____

_____

Requirement 2

ROE Analysis	Current Year	Prior Year
Net Income ⎯⎯⎯⎯⎯ Net Sales		
X Net Sales ⎯⎯⎯⎯⎯⎯⎯ Average Total Assets		
X Average Total Assets ⎯⎯⎯⎯⎯⎯⎯⎯⎯⎯⎯⎯ Average Shareholders' Equity		
Return on Equity		

_____

_____

_____

_____

_____

_____

_____

E5–19.

Requirement 1

	Current Year	Prior Year
Net income (given) Average Shareholders' Equity (given)		

_____
_____
_____

Requirement 2

ROE Analysis	Current Year	Prior Year
Net Income Sales		
X $\dfrac{\text{Net Sales}}{\text{Average Total Assets}}$		
X $\dfrac{\text{Average Total Assets}}{\text{Average Shareholders' Equity}}$		
Return on Equity		

_____
_____
_____
_____
_____
_____

Requirement 3

_____
_____
_____
_____
_____
_____
_____
_____
_____
_____
_____

Name _____ Date _____ Course _____ Section _____

P5–1.

(1) _____	(11) _____	(21) _____
(2) _____	(12) _____	(22) _____
(3) _____	(13) _____	(23) _____
(4) _____	(14) _____	
(5) _____	(15) _____	
(6) _____	(16) _____	
(7) _____	(17) _____	
(8) _____	(18) _____	
(9) _____	(19) _____	
(10) _____	(20) _____	

P5–2.

_____ (1) Retained earnings

_____ (2) Current liabilities

_____ (3) Liquidity

_____ (4) Contra-assets account

_____ (5) Accumulated depreciation

_____ (6) Intangible assets

_____ (7) Other assets

_____ (8) Shares outstanding

_____ (9) Normal operating cycle

_____ (10) Book Value

_____ (11) Capital in excess of par

_____ (12) Liabilities

_____ (13) Fixed assets

_____ (14) Shareholders' equity

_____ (15) Current assets

_____ (16) Assets

_____ (17) Long-term liabilities

P5–3.

Requirement 1

KING JEWELERS
Balance Sheet
At December 31, 2005

Assets

Liabilities

Stockholders' Equity

P5–3. (continued)
Requirement 2

Item	Computation of Net Book Value	Brief Explanation of Net Book Value

P5–4.
Requirement 1

STEWART COMPANY
Balance Sheet (Partial)
At December 31, 2005

Requirement 2

P5–5.

Requirement 1

MESA CORPORATION
Balance Sheet
At December 31, 2004

Stockholders' Equity						

Requirement 2

Name _____ Date _____ Course _____ Section _____

P5–6.

TOMMY HILFIGER CORPORATION
Consolidated Statement of Income
For the Period Ended March 31, 2001
(in thousands, except per share amounts)

©The McGraw-Hill Companies, Inc., 2004   209   Chapter 5

P5–7.

Requirement 1(a)

THOMAS REAL ESTATE COMPANY
Income Statement
For the Year Ended March 31, 2005

Requirement 1(b) appears on the following page.

Requirement 2

P5–7. (concluded)
Requirement 1(b)

THOMAS REAL ESTATE COMPANY
Balance Sheet
At March 31, 2005

Assets

Liabilities

Stockholders' Equity

P5–8.

SRINIVASAN COMPANY
Statement of Cash Flows
For the Year Ended December 31, 2004

NaNName _____ Date _____ Course _____ Section _____

P5–9.
Requirement 1

Transaction	Gross Profit	Operating Income (Loss)	Return on Equity
(a)			
(b)			
(c)			
(d)			

(a)

(b)

(c)

(d)

Requirement 2

P5–10.

ADOLF COORS COMPANY
Consolidated Statement of Income
For the Year Ended December 26
(in thousands)

P5–11.

Item	Key Computations Numbered in Order	Amount

AP5–1.

CARPET BAZAAR
Balance Sheet
At December 31, 2005

Assets

Liabilities

Stockholders' Equity

AP5–1. (continued)
Requirement 2

Item	Computation of Net Book Value	Brief Explanation of Net Book Value

AP5–2.
Requirement 1

RICHMOND, INC.
Balance Sheet (Partial)
At December 31, 2005

Requirement 2

AP5–3.

Requirement 1

POTAMIA CORPORATION
Balance Sheet
At December 31, 2004

Stockholders' Equity		

Requirement 2

AP5–4.

Requirement 1(a)

ACME PEST CONTROL SERVICES
Income Statement
For the Year Ended August 31, 2005

AP5–4. (concluded)

Requirement 1(b)

ACME PEST CONTROL SERVICE
Balance Sheet
For the Year Ended August 31, 2005

Assets						

Liabilities						

Stockholders' Equity						

Requirement 2

AP5–5.

Transaction	Operating Income (Loss)	Net Income	Return on Equity
(a)			
(b)			
(c)			
(d)			

_____
_____
_____
_____

(a)
_____
_____
_____
_____
_____
_____
_____

(b)
_____
_____
_____
_____

(c)
_____
_____
_____
_____

(d)
_____
_____
_____
_____

Requirement 2
_____
_____
_____
_____
_____
_____
_____
_____

Name _____ Date _____ Course _____ Section _____

CP5–1.

1. _____
_____

2. _____
_____
_____

3. _____
_____

4. _____
_____

5. _____
_____

6. _____
_____
_____

CP5–2.

1. _____
_____

2. _____
_____

3. _____
_____

4. _____
_____
_____

5. _____
_____
_____

6. _____
_____

7. _____
_____
_____
_____

CP5–3.

Requirement 1

	American Eagle Outfitters	Abercrombie & Fitch
Net income (given)		
Average Shareholders' Equity (given)		

_____
_____
_____
_____

Requirement 2

ROE Analysis	American Eagle Outfitters	Abercrombie & Fitch
$\dfrac{\text{Net Income}}{\text{Net Sales}}$		
$\times \dfrac{\text{Net Sales}}{\text{Average Total Assets}}$		
$\times \dfrac{\text{Average Total Assets}}{\text{Average Shareholders' Equity}}$		
Return on Equity		

_____
_____
_____
_____
_____
_____
_____
_____
_____
_____
_____

CP5–3. (continued)

Requirement 3

Industry Return on Equity (ROE) profit driver analysis:

ROE Analysis	Industry Average	American Eagle Outfitters	Abercrombie & Fitch
Net Profit Margin			
Asset Turnover			
Financial Leverage			
Return on Equity			

_____
_____
_____
_____
_____
_____
_____
_____
_____
_____

CP5–4.

_____
_____
_____
_____
_____
_____
_____
_____
_____
_____
_____
_____
_____
_____
_____
_____
_____
_____
_____
_____
_____
_____

CP5–5.

Item and Computation	Amount
(1) Gross margin on sales	
Computation:	
(2) EPS	
Computation:	
(3) Pretax income	
Computation:	
(4) Average sale price per share of stock	
Computation (and proof):	
(5) Beginning balance	
Computation:	

CP5–6.

CP5–7.
Requirement 1

Requirement 2

CP5–8.

Strategy Change	Current Period ROE	Future Periods' ROE	Explanation
a.			
b.			
c.			

CP5–9.

Error	Net Income		Assets		Liabilities	
	2003	2004	2003	2004	2003	2004
(1)						
(2)						
(3)						
(4)						
(5)						
(6)						
(7)						

CP5–9. (continued)

(1)

(2)

(3)

(4)

(5)

CP5–9. (continued)

(6) _____

_____
_____
_____
_____
_____
_____
_____
_____

(7) _____

_____
_____
_____
_____
_____
_____
_____
_____
_____

CP5–10.

1. _____

_____
_____
_____

2. _____

_____
_____
_____
_____
_____

3. _____

_____
_____
_____
_____
_____

CP5–11.

_____
_____
_____

E6–6.

Requirement 1

SLATE, INCORPORATED
Income Statement
For the Year Ended December 31, 2004

	Amount	Percentage Analysis

Requirement 2

Gross (profit) margin: _____

Gross profit percentage ratio: _____

_____

_____

_____

_____

_____

_____

_____

_____

_____

_____

_____

_____

_____

_____

_____

_____

_____

E6–7.

Requirement 1

WOLVERINE WORLD WIDE, INC.
Income Statement
For the Year Ended 2003

	Amount	Percentage Analysis

Requirement 2

Gross margin: _____

Gross margin ratio: _____

_____
_____
_____
_____
_____
_____
_____
_____
_____
_____
_____
_____
_____
_____
_____
_____
_____
_____

E6–17.

Requirement 1

Dec. 31, 2009						

Dec. 31, 2009						

Requirement 2

Requirement 3

E6–18.

Requirement 1

$$\text{Receivables turnover} = \frac{\text{Net Sales}}{\text{Average Net Trade Accounts Receivable}} = \underline{\hspace{2cm}} = $$

$$\text{Average days sales in receivable} = \frac{365}{\text{Receivables Turnover}} = \underline{\hspace{2cm}} = $$

Requirement 2

_____
_____
_____
_____
_____
_____
_____

E6–19.

Requirement 1

Requirement 2

$$\text{Receivables turnover} = \frac{\text{Net Sales}}{\text{Average Net Trade Account Receivable}} = \underline{\hspace{2cm}} = $$

Requirement 2

Requirement 3

_____
_____
_____
_____
_____
_____

E6–20.

Requirement 1

_____
_____
_____
_____
_____
_____
_____
_____
_____
_____

Requirement 2

a. _____
_____
_____
_____
_____

b. _____
_____
_____
_____
_____

E6–21.

Requirement 1

_____
_____
_____
_____
_____
_____
_____
_____
_____

Requirement 2

a. _____
_____
_____
_____

b. _____
_____
_____
_____
_____

E6–22.

Requirement 1

JONES COMPANY
Bank Reconciliation, June 30, 2004

Company's Books					Bank Statement				
Additions:					Additions:				
Deductions:					Deductions:				
Correct cash balance…					Correct cash balance…				

Requirement 2

Requirement 3

Requirement 4

P6–1.

Case A

_____

_____

_____

_____

_____

_____

_____

_____

_____

_____

_____

_____

Case B

_____

_____

_____

_____

_____

_____

_____

_____

_____

_____

_____

_____

_____

_____

_____

Case C

_____

_____

_____

_____

_____

_____

_____

_____

_____

_____

_____

_____

_____

_____

_____

_____

P6–2.

Requirement 1

	Sales Revenue	Sales Discounts (taken)	Sales Returns and Allowances	Bad Debt Expenses
(a)				
(b)				
(c)				
(d)				
(e)				
(f)				
(g)				
(h)				
(i)				
(j)				
(k)				
(l)				
(m)				
Total				

Computations:

_____

_____

_____

_____

_____

_____

_____

_____

Requirement 2

P6–3.

Income Statement Items	Ref.	Case A	Ref.	Case B

Computations:

CASE A	CASE B
a.	
b.	
c.	
d.	
e.	
f.	
g.	
h.	
i.	

P6–4.

1.

2.

Year 2					
Year 1					

Allowance for DA Year 2

Allowance for DA Year 1

P6–5.

Requirement 1   ***Aging Analysis of Accounts Receivable***

Customer	Total Receivables	(a) Not Yet Due	(b) Up to One Year Past Due	(c) More Then One Year Past Due
	%	%	%	%

Requirement 2   ***Estimated Amounts Uncollectible***

Age	Amount of Receivable	Estimated Loss Rate	Estimated Uncollectible
(a)		%	
(b)			
(c)			
Total			

Requirement 3

Requirement 4

P6–6.

Requirement 1

BUILDERS COMPANY, INC.
Income Statement
For the Year Ended December 31, 2006

Requirement 2

$$\text{Gross Profit Percentage} = \frac{\text{Gross Profit}}{\text{Net Sales}} = \underline{\hspace{3cm}} =$$

P6–7.

Requirement 1

		Projected change	No change from beginning of year
Receivables Turnover =	Net Sales / Average Net Trade Accounts Receivable	_____ =	_____ =

Requirement 2

_____
_____
_____
_____
_____
_____
_____
_____
_____

Requirement 3

_____
_____
_____
_____
_____
_____
_____
_____
_____
_____
_____
_____
_____
_____

P6–8.

Requirement 1

(a) _____

(b) _____

(c) _____

(d) _____

_____

_____

_____

Requirement 2

Basic Recommendations:

(1) _____

_____

_____

_____

_____

_____

_____

_____

_____

_____

_____

_____

_____

_____

(2) _____

_____

_____

_____

_____

_____

_____

_____

_____

_____

Name _____ Date _____ Course _____ Section _____

P6–9.
Requirement 1

HOPKINS COMPANY
Bank Reconciliation, April 30, 2006

Company's Books	Bank Statement
Additions:	Additions:
Deductions:	Deductions:
Correct cash balance...	Correct cash balance...

Requirement 2

(1)

(2)

(3)

Requirement 3

Requirement 4

P6–10.

Requirement 1

_____
_____
_____
_____

Requirement 2

_____
_____
_____
_____
_____
_____

Requirement 3

MARTHA COMPANY
Bank Reconciliation, August 31, 2004

Company's Books		Bank Statement	
Additions:		Additions:	
Deductions:		Deductions:	
Correct cash balance…		Correct cash balance…	

Requirement 4

(1)

(2)

P6–10. (continued)

Requirement 4 (concluded)

Requirement 5

Requirement 6

P6–11. (Based on Supplement A).

Requirement 1

(a)

(b)

(c)

(d)

(e)

(f)

(g)

(h)

P6–11. (continued)
Requirement 1 (concluded)

(i)

(j)

(k)

(l)

(m)

Requirement 2

AP6–1.

Requirement 1

	Sales Revenue	Sales Discounts (taken)	Sales Returns and Allowances	Bad Debt Expenses
(a)				
(b)				
(c)				
(d)				
(e)				
(f)				
(g)				
(h)				
(i)				
(j)				
(k)				
(l)				
(m)				
Total				

Computations:

_____

_____

_____

_____

_____

_____

_____

_____

Requirement 2

Income statement:

_____

_____

_____

_____

_____

_____

_____

_____

_____

_____

AP6–2.

1.

2.

Allowances for Doubtful Accounts and Discounts	Balance at Beginning of Year	Additions Charged to Costs and Expenses	Deductions from Reserve	Balance at End of Year
Year 3				
Year 2				
Year 1				

Year 3   Allowance for Doubtful Accounts

Year 2   Allowance for Doubtful Accounts

Year 1   Allowance for Doubtful Accounts

AP6–3.

Requirement 1　　　　　　　**Aging Analysis of Accounts Receivable**

Customer	Total Receivables	(a) Not Yet Due	(b) Up to 6 Months Past Due	(c) Up to 6-12 Mo. Past Due	(d) More Than 12 Mo. Past Due
R. Devens					
C. Howard					
D. McClain					
T. Skibinski					
H. Wu					
Totals					
Percent	%	%	%	%	%

Requirement 2　　　　　　　**Estimated Amounts Uncollectible**

Age	Amount of Receivable	Estimated Loss Rate	Estimated Uncollectible
(a) Not yet due		%	
(b) Up to 6 months past due			
(c) 6 to 12 months past due			
(d) Over 12 months past due			
Total			

Requirement 3

To adjust for estimated bad debt loss:

Requirement 4

Income Statement:

Balance Sheet:
Current Assets:

Name _____ Date _____ Course _____ Section _____

AP6–4.

Requirement 1

BIG TOMMY CORPORATION
Income Statement
For the Year Ended December 31, 2009

Requirement 2

Gross Profit Percentage = $\dfrac{\text{Gross Profit}}{\text{Net Sales}}$ = _____ =

AP6–5.

Requirement 1

Requirement 2

Requirement 3

PACKER COMPANY
Bank Reconciliation, December 31, 2004

Company's Books		Bank Statement	
Additions:		Additions:	
Deductions:		Deductions:	
Correct cash balance…		Correct cash balance…	

Requirement 4

(1)

(2)

(3)

AP6–5. (continued)
Requirement 4 (concluded)

Requirement 5

Requirement 6

Balance Sheet (2004):
   Current Assets:

CP6–1.

1. _____
_____
_____
_____
_____
_____
_____
_____
_____

2. _____
_____
_____
_____
_____
_____
_____
_____
_____
_____

3.

		2000	1999
Gross Profit Percentage	= $\dfrac{\text{Gross Profit}}{\text{Net Sales}}$	_____ =	_____ =

_____
_____
_____
_____
_____
_____

4. _____
_____
_____
_____
_____
_____
_____
_____

CP6–2.

1. _____
_____
_____
_____
_____
_____
_____
_____

2. _____
_____
_____
_____
_____

3.

$$\text{Receivables turnover} = \frac{\text{Net Sales}}{\text{Average Net Trade Accounts Receivable}} = \underline{\hspace{2cm}} = $$

_____
_____
_____
_____

4. _____
_____
_____
_____
_____
_____
_____

CP6–3.

1.

Current year	Abercrombie & Fitch	American Eagle Outfitters
Gross Profit Percentage $= \dfrac{\text{Gross Profit}}{\text{Net Sales}}$	————— =	————— =

Prior year	Abercrombie & Fitch	American Eagle Outfitters
Gross Profit Percentage $= \dfrac{\text{Gross Profit}}{\text{Net Sales}}$	————— =	————— =

_____
_____
_____
_____
_____
_____

2. _____
_____
_____
_____
_____
_____
_____
_____
_____

3. _____

	Industry Average	Abercrombie & Fitch	American Eagle Outfitters
Gross Profit Percentage =			

_____
_____
_____

4. _____

Abercrombie & Fitch	2000	1999
Receivables turnover $= \dfrac{\text{Net Sales}}{\substack{\text{Average Net Trade} \\ \text{Accounts Receivable}}}$	————— =	————— =

_____
_____
_____
_____

CP6–4.

CP6–5.

1.

_____
_____
_____
_____
_____
_____
_____
_____
_____

2.

$$\text{Receivables turnover} = \frac{\text{Net Sales}}{\text{Average Net Trade Accounts Receivable}} = \rule{3cm}{0.4pt} =$$

3.

	Trade debtors	*Other debtors*
$\dfrac{\text{Provision for doubtful Debts}}{\text{Trade receivables}}$	_____ =	_____ =

_____
_____
_____
_____
_____
_____
_____

4.

Allowance for Doubtful Accounts

CP6–6.

Requirement 1

CP6–6. (continued)

Requirement 2

_____
_____
_____
_____
_____
_____
_____
_____
_____
_____
_____
_____
_____
_____
_____
_____
_____
_____
_____
_____
_____
_____
_____
_____
_____
_____
_____
_____
_____
_____
_____

Name _____ Date _____ Course _____ Section _____

CP6–7.

1.

2.

3.

4.

CP6–8.

1. _____

2. _____

3. _____

4. _____

5. _____

CP6–9.

M7–1.

Type of Inventory	Type of Business	
	Merchandising	Manufacturing
Merchandise	_____	_____
Finished goods	_____	_____
Work in process	_____	_____
Raw materials	_____	_____

M7–2.

M7–3.

	(a) Part of inventory	(b) Expenses as incurred
1. Wages of factory workers		
2. Sales salaries		
3. Cost of raw materials purchased		
4. Heat, light and power for the factory building		
5. Heat, light and power for the headquarters office building		

M7–4.

M7–5.

(a)	Rising costs
	Highest net income
	Highest inventory
(b)	Declining costs
	Highest net income
	Highest inventory

M7–6.

(a)	Rising costs	
(b)	Declining costs	

M7–7.

	Quantity	Cost per item	Replacement cost per item	Lower of cost or market	Total reported
Item A					
Item B					
Total					

M7–8.

_____ (a) Parts inventory delivered daily by suppliers instead of weekly.

_____ (b) Shorten production process from 10 days to 8 days

_____ (c) Extend payments for inventory purchases from 15 days to 30 days.

M7–9.

_____

_____

_____

_____

_____

_____

_____

_____

E7–1.

Case	Sales Revenue	Beginning Inventory	Purchases	Total Available	Ending Inventory	Cost of Goods Sold	Gross Profit	Expenses	Pretax Income or (Loss)
A	$	$	$	$	$	$	$	$	$
B									
C									
D									
E									

E7–2.

	Case A	Case B	Case C
Sales revenue			
Sales returns and allowances			
Net sales revenue			
Beginning inventory			
Purchases			
Goods available for sale			
Ending inventory			
Cost of goods sold			
Gross profit			
Expenses			
Pretax income			

E7–3.

E7–4.

Requirement 1

LUNAR COMPANY
Income Statement
For the Year Ended December 31, 2004

	Case A FIFO									Case B LIFO								
Sales revenue	$									$								
Cost of goods sold:																		
Goods available for sale																		
Cost of goods sold																		
Gross margin																		
Expenses																		
Pretax income																		

Computations:

_____
_____
_____
_____
_____

Requirement 2

_____
_____
_____
_____
_____
_____
_____

Requirement 3

_____
_____
_____
_____
_____
_____

E7–5.

Requirement 1

SCORESBY INC.
Income Statement
For the Year Ended December 31, 2006

	Case A FIFO						Case B LIFO					
Sales revenue	$						$					
Cost of goods sold:												
Beginning inventory												
Purchases												
Goods available for sale												
Ending inventory												
Cost of goods sold												
Gross profit												
Expenses												
Pretax income												

Computations:

_____
_____
_____
_____
_____
_____
_____
_____
_____
_____
_____
_____
_____
_____
_____
_____
_____

Requirement 2
_____
_____
_____
_____
_____
_____
_____
_____
_____

Requirement 3
_____
_____
_____
_____
_____
_____
_____

E7–6.

Requirement 1

Income Statement	Units		Inventory Costing Method		
			FIFO	LIFO	Weighted Average

Computations:

_____

_____

_____

_____

_____

_____

Requirement 2

_____

_____

_____

_____

_____

_____

_____

_____

_____

_____

_____

_____

_____

_____

_____

Requirement 3

_____

_____

_____

E7–7.

Requirement 1

	FIFO	LIFO	Weighted Average

Computations:

_____

_____

_____

_____

_____

_____

_____

_____

_____

_____

_____

_____

_____

_____

Requirement 2

	FIFO	LIFO	Weighted Average

E7–7. (concluded)

Requirement 3

_____

_____

_____

_____

_____

_____

_____

_____

_____

_____

_____

_____

_____

E7–8.

1. _____

_____

_____

_____

_____

_____

_____

2. _____

_____

_____

_____

_____

_____

_____

E7–9.

Item	Quantity	Total Cost		Total Market		LCM Valuation
A		x $_____ =		x $_____ =		
B		x =		x =		
C		x =		x =		
D		x =		x =		
E		x =		x =		
	Total					

E7–10.

Requirement 1

Item	Quantity	Total Cost		Total Market		LCM Valuation
A		x $ _____ =		x $ _____ =		
B		x =		x =		
C		x =		x =		
D		x =		x =		
	Total					

_____

_____

_____

_____

Requirement 2

_____

_____

_____

_____

_____

_____

_____

_____

_____

_____

_____

_____

E7–11.

Requirement 1

$$\text{Inventory turnover} = \frac{\text{Cost of Goods Sold}}{\text{Average Inventory}} = \text{_____} =$$

Average days to sell inventory = _____

Requirement 2

_____

_____

_____

_____

_____

_____

_____

_____

_____

E7–12.

CASE A—FIFO:

Inventory turnover $\;=\;\dfrac{\text{Cost of Goods Sold}}{\text{Average Inventory}}\;=\;$ _____ $\;=\;$

CASE B—LIFO:

Inventory turnover $\;=\;\dfrac{\text{Cost of Goods Sold}}{\text{Average Inventory}}\;=\;$ _____ $\;=\;$

Name _____ Date _____ Course _____ Section _____

E7–13.

	Current Year	Previous Year	Change
Inventory	_____	– _____	= _____
A/P	_____	– _____	= _____

_____
_____
_____
_____
_____
_____
_____
_____

E7–14.

1. _____
_____
_____
_____
_____
_____
_____
_____

2. _____
_____
_____
_____
_____
_____
_____
_____
_____
_____

3. _____
_____
_____
_____

4. _____
_____
_____
_____

E7–15.

Requirement 1

_____

_____

_____

_____

_____

_____

_____

_____

_____

_____

_____

_____

_____

_____

_____

_____

_____

_____

Requirement 2

Account	Year of Error	Subsequent Year
Beginning inventory		
Cost of goods sold		
Ending inventory		
Net income		
Retained earnings		
Taxes payable		

E7–16.

Requirement 1

_____

_____

_____

_____

_____

_____

_____

_____

_____

_____

Requirement 2

_____

_____

_____

_____

_____

_____

Requirement 3

	First Quarter	Second Quarter

Requirement 4

	First Quarter			Second Quarter		
	Incorrect	Correct	Error	Incorrect	Correct	Error
Beginning inventory	$	$		$	$	
Ending inventory						
Cost of goods sold						
Gross profit						
Pretax income						

E7–17. (Supplement A)

Requirement 1

_____
_____
_____
_____
_____
_____
_____
_____
_____
_____
_____
_____
_____
_____
_____
_____
_____
_____
_____
_____
_____

Requirement 2

_____
_____
_____
_____
_____
_____
_____
_____
_____

E7–18. (Supplement B)

Requirement 1

Requirement 2

Requirement 3

Requirement 4

Requirement 5

Requirement 6

E7–19. (Supplement C)

CASE A: Perpetual inventory system:

January 14			
April 9			
September 2			
End of year			

CASE B: Periodic inventory system:

January 14			
April 9			
September 2			
End of year			

P7–1.

Item	Amount	Explanation
Ending inventory (physical count on December 31, 2004)		
(a)		
(b)		
(c)		
(d)		
(e)		
(f)		
(g)		
Correct inventory, December 31, 2004		

P7–2.

(a) Goods available for sale for all methods:

	Units	Unit Cost	Total Cost

Ending inventory: _____

(b) and (c)

(1) Weighted average cost:	

(2) First-in, first-out:	

(3) Last-in, first-out:	

(4) Specific identification:	

P7–3.

Requirement 1

ATLANTA COMPANY
Partial Income Statement
For the Month Ended January 31, 2004

	(a) Weighted Average	(b) FIFO	(c) LIFO	(d) Specific Identification
Sales revenue				
Cost of goods sold				
Gross profit				

Computations:

	Units	Weighted Average	FIFO	LIFO	Specific Identification

Requirement 2

_____
_____
_____
_____
_____

Requirement 3

_____
_____
_____

Requirement 4

_____
_____
_____
_____
_____

P7–4.

Requirement 1

Requirement 2

Requirement 3

P7–5.

Requirement 1

	Prices Rising		Prices Falling	
	FIFO	LIFO	FIFO	LIFO

Requirement 2

Requirement 3

Requirement 4

P7–6.

Requirement 1

	Impact on GM net income (in millions)

Requirement 2

Requirement 3

P7–7.
Requirement 1

SMART COMPANY
Income Statement (LCM Basis)
For the Year Ended December 31, 2004

Item	Quantity	Original Cost		Replacement Cost (Market)		LCM Valuation
		Per Unit	Total	Per Unit	Total	
A						
B						
C						
D						
Total						

Requirement 2

Item Changed	FIFO Cost Basis	LCM Basis	Amount of Change (Decrease)

Analysis:

P7–7. (continued)

Requirement 3

_____

_____

_____

_____

_____

_____

_____

_____

_____

_____

_____

_____

_____

_____

_____

_____

_____

_____

_____

_____

Requirement 4

_____

_____

_____

_____

_____

_____

_____

_____

_____

_____

_____

_____

_____

_____

_____

_____

_____

_____

P7–8.

Requirement 1

	Projected change	No change from beginning of year
Inventory Turnover $=$ $\dfrac{\text{Cost of Goods Sold}}{\text{Average Inventory}}$	_____ $=$	_____ $=$

Requirement 2

_____
_____
_____
_____
_____
_____
_____
_____
_____

Requirement 3

_____
_____
_____
_____
_____
_____
_____
_____
_____
_____
_____
_____

P7–9.

Requirement 1

CLEMENT COMPANY
Income Statement Corrected

	2003	2004	2005	2006
Sales revenue				
Cost of goods sold				
Gross margin				
Expenses				
Pretax income				

Requirement 2

Computation	2003	2004	2005	2006
Gross profit ratio:				
Before correction:				
After correction:				

Requirement 3

	2004	2005
Before correction:		
2004:		
2005:		
After correction:		
2004:		
2005:		
Difference		

P7–10. (Supplement A)

1. _____

2. _____

P7–11. (Supplement B)

(a)

(b)

(c)

(d)

P7–11. (Supplement B) (concluded)

(e)											
(f)											
(g)											
(h)											
(i)											

AP7–1.

(a) Goods available for sale for all methods:

	Units	Unit Cost	Total Cost

Ending inventory: _____

(b) and (c)

(1) Weighted average cost:	

(2) First-in, first-out:	

(3) Last-in, first-out:	

(4) Specific identification:	

AP7–2.

The computations for Daimler Chrysler are shown below:

Requirement 1

_____

_____

_____

_____

_____

_____

_____

_____

_____

_____

Requirement 2

_____

_____

_____

_____

_____

_____

_____

_____

_____

_____

_____

_____

Requirement 3

_____

_____

_____

_____

_____

_____

_____

_____

_____

_____

AP7–3.

Requirement 1

		Projected change	No change from beginning of year
Inventory Turnover	$=\dfrac{\text{Cost of Goods Sold}}{\text{Average Inventory}}$	_____ =	_____ =

Requirement 2

Projected increase in inventory = _____

_____

_____

_____

_____

_____

_____

_____

Requirement 3

_____

_____

_____

_____

_____

_____

_____

_____

_____

_____

_____

_____

_____

AP7–4.

Requirement 1

	2003	2004	2005	2006

Requirement 2

_____
_____
_____
_____
_____
_____
_____
_____
_____
_____
_____
_____
_____
_____

Requirement 3

	2004	2005

CP7–1.

1. _____
_____
_____
_____
_____
_____
_____
_____

2. _____
_____
_____
_____
_____
_____
_____
_____
_____

Cost of goods sold	_____
+ Ending inventory	_____
− Beginning inventory	_____
Purchases	_____

Inventory

Beg. Balance

End. Balance

3. _____
_____
_____
_____
_____
_____
_____

4. _____
_____
_____
_____
_____
_____
_____

CP7–2.

1. _____

_____

_____

_____

_____

_____

2. _____

_____

_____

_____

_____

_____

_____

3.

$$\text{Inventory turnover} = \frac{\text{Cost of Goods Sold}}{\text{Average Inventory}} = \underline{\hspace{2cm}} =$$

Name _____ Date _____ Course _____ Section _____

CP7–3.

1.

	Abercrombie & Fitch	American Eagle Outfitters
Inventory Turnover $= \dfrac{\text{Cost of Goods Sold}}{\text{Average Inventory}}$	_____ =	_____ =

_____
_____
_____
_____
_____
_____
_____
_____
_____
_____
_____
_____
_____
_____
_____
_____
_____
_____
_____

2.

	Industry Average	Abercrombie & Fitch	American Eagle Outfitters
Inventory Turnover $=$			

_____
_____
_____
_____
_____
_____
_____
_____
_____
_____
_____

Name _____ Date _____ Course _____ Section _____

CP7–4.

CP7–5.

The following points can be discussed: _____

1. _____

_____

2. _____

_____

3. _____

_____

4. _____

_____

5. _____

_____

6. _____

_____

7. _____

_____

_____

_____

_____

_____

CP7–6.

1. _____

_____

_____

_____

_____

_____

_____

2. _____

_____

_____

_____

_____

_____

_____

Name _____ Date _____ Course _____ Section _____

CP7–7.
Requirement 1

	1995	1994	1993
Caterpillar			

1995 LIFO

   Inventory turnover = ———————— = ———

1995 FIFO

   Inventory turnover = ———————— = ———

1994 LIFO

   Inventory turnover = ———————— = ———

1994 FIFO

   Inventory turnover = ———————— = ———

DEERE

1995 LIFO   ———————

1995 FIFO   ———————

CP7–7. (continued)

Requirement 2

Requirement 3

CP7–8. (Supplement A)

Requirement 1

Requirement 2

Requirement 3

CP7–9.

CP7–10.

To: _____

From: _____

Re: _____

1. _____
_____
_____
_____
_____
_____
_____

2. _____
_____
_____
_____
_____
_____
_____
_____

3. _____
_____
_____
_____
_____
_____
_____
_____
_____

4. _____
_____
_____
_____
_____
_____

CP7–11.
_____
_____
_____
_____
_____
_____
_____

Chapter 7

E8–5.

Requirement 1

Date	Assets	Liabilities	Stockholders' Equity
January 1			
January 2			
January 3			
January 5			
July 1			

Requirement 2

Acquisition cost of the machine:

Requirement 3

Requirement 4

Requirement 5 (end of 2004)

E8–6.

Requirement 1 (2003):

Requirement 2 (2004):

Requirement 3 (2004):

E8–7.

Requirement 1

Date	Assets		Liabilities		Stockholders' Equity	
1. 2003						
2. 2004						

1. _____

E8–14.

Requirement 1

	Assets		Liabilities		Stockholders' Equity	
a.						
b.						
c.						

Requirement 2

Summarization of the effects of the disposal: _____

1. _____

_____

_____

_____

_____

_____

2. _____

_____

_____

_____

_____

3. _____

_____

_____

_____

E8–15.

Requirement 1

_____

_____

_____

Requirement 2

December 31, 2004:

E8–16.

Requirement 1

Computation of acquisition cost of the deposit in 2003:

Requirement 2

Computation of depletion for 2003:

Requirement 3

Computation of acquisition cost of the deposit in 2004:

E8–17.

Requirement 1
Acquisition cost:

Requirement 2
Amortization on December 31, 2004:

Requirement 3
Income statement for 2004:

Balance sheet at December 31, 2004:

E8–18.

Requirement 1 (January 1, 2004):

Requirement 2 (Adjusting entry on December 31, 2004):

E8–19.

Item	Location
1. The detail on major classifications of long-lived assets	
2. The accounting method(s) used for financial reporting purposes.	
3. Whether the company has had any capital expenditures for the year.	
4. Net amount of property, plant and equipment.	
5. Policies on amortizing intangibles.	
6. Depreciation expense.	
7. Any significant gains or losses on disposals of fixed assets.	
8. Prior year's accumulated depreciation.	
9. The amount of assets written off as impaired during the year.	

E8–20.

December 31, 2004:

Adjusting entry for 2004 depreciation:

E8–21.

Requirement 1

Date	Assets			Liabilities			Stockholders' Equity		
2004									

E8–22.

Requirement 1

Requirement 2

Age of Machine A at December 31, 2003:

Requirement 3

Computations:

Requirement 4

E8–23.

Requirement 1

_____

_____

_____

_____

Requirement 2

Depreciation expense after the change in estimates:

Step 1 –

_____

_____

_____

Step 2 –

_____

_____

_____

_____

Step 3 –

_____

_____

_____

_____

_____

_____

_____

_____

_____

_____

_____

_____

_____

_____

Requirement 3

_____

_____

_____

_____

_____

_____

_____

_____

_____

_____

_____

_____

P8–1.
Requirement 1
_____
_____
_____
_____
_____
_____
_____

Requirement 2

Date	Assets						Liabilities						Stockholders' Equity					
Jan. 2																		
Jan. 15																		

Computations:
(1) Equipment: _____
_____
_____
_____
_____

(2) Balance payable: _____
_____
_____
_____

(3) Common stock: _____
_____

(4) Additional paid-in capital: _____
_____
_____

Requirement 3
_____
_____
_____
_____
_____
_____
_____
_____
_____
_____

334

P8–2.

Requirement 1

_____
_____
_____
_____
_____
_____
_____

Requirement 2

On January 2, 2003:

On January 15, 2003:

Computations:

(1) Equipment:
_____

(2) Balance payable:
_____

(3) Common stock:
_____

(4) Additional paid-in capital:
_____

Requirement 3

_____
_____
_____
_____
_____
_____
_____

P8–3.

Requirement 1

	Building	Accumulated Depreciation	Depreciation Expense	Repairs Expense	Cash
Balance 1/1/2004	$ 4 2 0 0 0 0				
Depreciation					
Balance prior to expenditures	4 2 0 0 0 0				
a.					
b.					
c.					
Balance 12/31/2004					

Computations:

Requirement 2
Book Value of Building:

Requirement 3

P8–6.
Requirement 1
a. Straight-Line:

Year	Computation	Depreciation Expense	Accumulated Depreciation	Net Book Value
At acquisition				
1				
2				

b. Units of production:

Year	Computation	Depreciation Expense	Accumulated Depreciation	Net Book Value
At acquisition				
1				
2				

c. Double declining balance:

Year	Computation	Depreciation Expense	Accumulated Depreciation	Net Book Value
At acquisition				
1				
2				

Requirement 2
Cash Flow –

Fixed asset turnover –

EPS –

P8–7.

Requirement 1

Machine A – Jan. 1, 2003:																	
(a)																	
(b)																	
Machine B – December 31, 2003:																	
(a)																	
(b)																	
Machine C – January 1, 2003:																	
(a)																	
(b)																	

Requirement 2

Machine A

Machine B

Machine C

P8–8.

Fixed Assets		Accumulated Depreciation

Requirement 2

Requirement 3

P8–9.

Requirement 1

Date	Assets	Liabilities	Stockholders' Equity
Jan. 1			
Jan. 1			
Dec. 31			
2005			
Dec. 31			
Dec. 31			

Computations for Machine A:

(1)

(2)

(3)

P8–9. (continued)

Requirement 2   December 31, 2005 depreciation and amortization:

Patents:

Goodwill:

Leasehold improvements:

Machine A:

Machine B:

P8–10.

Requirement 1

January 5, 2003:

Requirement 2

December 31, 2003:

(a)

(b)

P8–11.

Requirement 1

a. _____

_____

b. _____

_____

c. _____

_____

_____

d. _____

_____

e. _____

_____

_____

Requirement 2

	Item	Date Acquired	Book Value Computations	Book Value Dec. 31, 2004
a.				
b.				
c.				
d.				
e.				
	Total book value			

Requirement 3

_____

_____

_____

_____

_____

_____

P8–12.

Requirement 1

(a)

(b)

Requirement 2

Requirement 3

December 31, 2004—Adjusting entry:

AP8–1.

Requirement 1

_____
_____
_____
_____
_____
_____
_____
_____
_____
_____
_____

Requirement 2

Date	Assets	Liabilities	Stockholders' Equity
June 1			
Sept. 2			

Computations:

_____
_____
_____
_____
_____
_____
_____
_____
_____
_____
_____
_____
_____
_____

Requirement 3

_____
_____
_____
_____
_____
_____
_____
_____
_____
_____
_____

AP8–2.

Requirement 1

_____
_____
_____
_____
_____
_____

Requirement 2

On June 1, 2002:			

On September 2, 2002:			

Computations:

(1) Equipment: _____

(2) Balance payable: _____
_____

(3) Common stock: _____
_____

(4) Additional paid-in capital: _____

(5) Interest expense: _____
_____

Requirement 3

_____
_____
_____
_____
_____
_____
_____

AP8–3.

Requirement 1

	Building	Accumulated Depreciation	Depreciation Expense	Repairs Expense	Cash
Balance 1/1/2005	$ 2 3 0 0 0 0				
Depreciation for 2005					
Balance prior to expenditures	2 3 0 0 0 0				
a.					
b.					
c.					
Balance 12/31/2005					

(1)

Requirement 2
Book Value of Building:

Requirement 3

AP8–4.

Requirement 1

Cost of each machine:

	Machine			Total
	A	B	C	

Requirement 2

Machine	Method	Computation
A	Straight-line	
B	Units-of-production	
C	200% declining balance	

Adjusting entry:

AP8–5.

Requirement 1

Accumulated Depreciation

Requirement 2

_____

_____

_____

_____

_____

_____

_____

_____

_____

_____

_____

_____

_____

_____

Ratio	Computation	Effect on Ratio of Failing to Record Depreciation Expense
Earnings per share	$\dfrac{\text{Net income}}{\text{Number of shares of stock outstanding}}$	
Fixed asset turnover	$\dfrac{\text{Sales}}{\text{Average net fixed asset balance}}$	
Financial leverage	$\dfrac{\text{Total assets}}{\text{Total stockholders' equity}}$	
Return on equity	$\dfrac{\text{Net income}}{\text{Average stockholders' equity}}$	

AP8–6.

Requirement 1

Machine A – Jan. 1, 2003:

(a)

(b)

Machine B – December 31, 2003:

(a)

(b)

Machine C – January 1, 2003:

(a)

(b)

Requirement 2

Machine A – Jan. 1, 2003:

Machine B – December 31, 2003:

Machine C – January 1, 2003:

AP8–7.

Requirement 1

Date	Assets	Liabilities	Stockholders' Equity
Jan. 1			
Jan. 1			
July 1			
Dec. 31			
2004			
Dec. 31			

Computations for Acquisition:

(1)

Name _____ Date _____ Course _____ Section_____

AP8–7. (continued)

Requirement 1 (continued)

Computations for Machine A:

(2)

(3)

(4)

AP8–7. (continued)

Requirement 2 December 31, 2004 depreciation and amortization expense:

License:

Leasehold improvements:

Goodwill:

Machine A:

Machine B:

AP8–8.

Requirement 1

a. _____

_____

_____

b. _____

_____

_____

c. _____

_____

_____

_____

d. _____

_____

_____

e. _____

_____

_____

Requirement 2

	Item	Date Acquired	Book Value Computations	Book Value Jan. 1, 2005
a.				
b.				
c.				
d.				
e.				
	Total book value			

Requirement 3

_____

_____

_____

_____

_____

_____

_____

_____

_____

CP8–1.

1. _____

2. _____

3. _____

4. _____

5. _____

6. _____

7. _____

CP8–2.

1.

2.

3.

4.

5.

6.

7.

CP8–3.

Requirement 1

	Abercrombie & Fitch	American Eagle
<u>Net fixed assets</u> Total assets	_____ =	_____ =

_____

_____

_____

_____

_____

_____

Requirement 2

	Abercrombie & Fitch	American Eagle
<u>Accumulated depreciation</u> Fixed assets (at cost)	_____ =	_____ =

_____

_____

_____

_____

_____

Requirement 3

	Abercrombie & Fitch	American Eagle
<u>Net sales</u> Average net fixed assets	_____ =	_____ =

_____

_____

_____

_____

_____

Requirement 4

_____

_____

_____

_____

_____

_____

_____

_____

CP8–4.

Industry	Company Name (Symbol, if Available)
1. Airline	
2. Hotels & Motels	
3. Footwear	
4. Computer Hardware	

CP8–5.

Requirement 1

Requirement 2

Company	Write-down

CP8–6.

Requirement 1

Requirement 2

CP8–7.

Requirement 1

Requirement 2

CP8–8.

Requirement 1

Requirement 2

Requirement 3

Chapter 8

Name _____ Date _____ Course _____ Section _____

CP8–8. (continued)
Requirement 4

_____

Requirement 5

_____

CP8–9.
(in mllions)

Property, Plant and Equipment		Accumulated Depreciation	

CP8–10.

_____
_____
_____
_____
_____
_____
_____
_____
_____
_____
_____
_____
_____
_____
_____
_____
_____
_____
_____
_____
_____
_____

CP8–11.

Requirement 1

_____
_____
_____
_____
_____
_____
_____
_____
_____

Requirement 2

_____
_____
_____
_____
_____
_____
_____
_____
_____
_____

CP8–12.

Requirement 1
_____
_____
_____
_____
_____
_____

Requirement 2
_____
_____
_____
_____
_____
_____
_____

Requirement 3
_____
_____
_____
_____
_____
_____
_____
_____

Requirement 4
_____
_____
_____
_____
_____
_____
_____

Requirement 5
_____
_____
_____
_____
_____
_____

CP8–13.
_____
_____
_____
_____
_____

M9–1.

2003 _____

2004 _____

_____

M9–2.

November 1, 2003:																			
December 31, 2003:																			

M9–3.

1. _____
2. _____
3. _____
4. _____
5. _____

M9–4.

_____

_____

_____

_____

M9–5.

Current Ratio	Working Capital
a.	
b.	
c.	
d.	

     Chapter 9

M9–6.

2003 _____
_____

2004 _____
_____

2005 _____
_____

2006 _____
_____

2007 _____
_____
_____

M9–7. _____
_____
_____

M9–8. _____
_____
_____

M9–9. _____
_____
_____
_____
_____
_____

M9–10. _____
_____
_____
_____
_____

M9–11. _____
_____
_____
_____
_____

E9–1.

Requirement 1

(a) Current assets																		
Current liabilities																		
Accounts payable																		

(b) Current ratio																		

Requirement 2

E9–2.
Requirement 1

Requirement 2

Requirement 3

Requirement 4

E9–3.

Requirement 1

Date	Assets	Liabilities	Stockholders' Equity
November 1, 2003			
December 31, 2003			
April 30, 2004			

Requirement 2

_____
_____
_____
_____
_____
_____
_____
_____
_____
_____
_____
_____
_____
_____
_____
_____
_____
_____

E9–4.

Requirement 1

Requirement 2

Requirement 3

Requirement 4

E9–7.

E9–8.

E9–9.

Requirement 1

(a)

_____

_____

_____

_____

_____

(b)

_____

_____

_____

_____

_____

Requirement 2

	2003	2004
Income Statement:		
Income tax expense		
Balance Sheet:		
Liabilities		
Deferred income tax		
Income tax payable		

Requirement 3

_____

_____

_____

_____

_____

_____

_____

_____

_____

Name _____ Date _____ Course _____ Section _____

E9–10.
Requirement 1
(a)
_____
_____
_____
_____
_____

(b)
_____
_____
_____
_____

Requirement 2

	2003	2004

Requirement 3

	2003	2004
Income Statement:		
Income tax expense		
Balance Sheet:		
Assets		
Deferred Income Tax		
Liabilities		
Deferred income tax		
Income tax payable		

Requirement 4
_____
_____
_____
_____
_____
_____
_____
_____
_____

E9–11.

Requirement 1

_____
_____
_____
_____
_____
_____
_____
_____
_____

Requirement 2

_____
_____
_____
_____
_____

Requirement 3

_____
_____
_____
_____
_____
_____

E9–12.

_____
_____
_____
_____
_____
_____
_____
_____
_____
_____
_____
_____
_____
_____
_____
_____
_____
_____

E9–13.

Requirement 1
_____
_____
_____

Requirement 2
_____
_____
_____

Requirement 3
_____
_____
_____

Requirement 4
_____
_____
_____

E9–14.

Requirement 1
_____
_____
_____

Requirement 2
_____
_____
_____

Requirement 3
  2003: _____
_____
  2004: _____
_____

E9–15.

Requirement 1

_____

_____

Requirement 2

Requirement 3

_____

_____

Requirement 4

	December 31	
	2003	2004

Computations:

_____

_____

_____

_____

P9–2.

Requirement 1

Date	Assets	Liabilities	Stockholders' Equity
January 8, 2004			
January 17, 2004			
April 1, 2004			
June 3, 2004			
July 5, 2004			
August 1, 2004			
December 20, 2004			
December 31, 2004			

Requirement 2

Transaction	Effect
January 8	
January 17	
April 1	
June 3	
July 5	
August 1	
December 20	
December 31	

Requirement 3

Transaction	Effect
January 8	
January 17	
April 1	
June 3	
July 5	
August 1	
December 20	
December 31	

P9–3.

Requirement 1

(a)

(b)

Requirement 2

(a)

(b)

Requirement 3

P9–3. (continued)

Requirement 4

_____

_____

_____

_____

_____

_____

_____

_____

_____

_____

_____

_____

_____

P9–4.

Requirement 1

Date	Assets	Liabilities	Stockholders' Equity
December 31, 2004			
January 6, 2005			
December 10, 2004			
December 31, 2004			

Requirement 2

_____

_____

_____

_____

_____

_____

_____

_____

_____

_____

_____

_____

_____

_____

_____

_____

P9–5.

1.

2003:

2004:

2.

2003:

2004:

3.

4.

5.

P9–6.

(a) _____

(b) _____

(c) _____

(d) _____

(e) _____

(f) _____

(g) _____

(h) _____

(i) _____

P9–7.

P9–8.

Requirement 1

(a)

(b)

Requirement 2

Requirement 3

Income Statement:

    Income Tax Expense

Balance Sheet:

    Deferred Income Tax Liability

    Income Tax Payable

P9–9.

Requirement 1

Balance in the fund:

_____

_____

Interest revenue:

_____

_____

Requirement 2

Single sum to deposit:

_____

_____

Interest revenue:

_____

_____

Requirement 3

Required amount to each equal annual deposit:

_____

_____

Interest revenue:

_____

_____

Requirement 4

Equal annual payments on note payable:

_____

_____

Interest expense:

_____

_____

P9–10.

_____

_____

_____

_____

_____

_____

_____

_____

_____

_____

_____

_____

_____

_____

_____

P9–11.

Requirement 1

Requirement 2

Requirement 3

2003:		
2004:		
2005:		
2006:		
Total interest revenue		

Requirement 4

(a) December 31, 2003:

	2004	2005
(b) December 31:		

(c) December 31, 2006:

Requirement 5

Income Statement, for the Year Ended December 31, 2004:	

Balance Sheet at December 31, 2004:	
Investments and Funds:	

AP9–1.

Requirement 1

January 15, 2004:		
January 31, 2004:		
April 30, 2004:		
June 3, 2004:		
July 5, 2004:		
August 31, 2004:		

Requirement 2

December 31, 2004:		
December 31, 2004:		
December 31, 2004:		

AP9–1. (continued)

Requirement 3

Balance Sheet:								
Current Liabilities								
Total Current Liabilities								

Requirement 4

Cash from Operating Activities:

Transaction	Effect
January 15, 2004	
January 31, 2004	
April 30, 2004	
June 3, 2004	
July 5, 2004	
August 31, 2004	
December 31, 2004	
December 31, 2004	
December 31, 2004	

AP9–2.

Requirement 1

Date	Assets	Liabilities	Stockholders' Equity
January 15, 2004			
January 31, 2004			
April 30, 2004			
June 3, 2004			
July 5, 2004			
August 31, 2004			
December 31, 2004			
December 31, 2004			
December 31, 2004			

Requirement 2

Cash from Operating Activities:

Transaction	Effect
January 15, 2004	
January 31, 2004	
April 30, 2004	
June 3, 2004	
July 5, 2004	
August 31, 2004	
December 31, 2004	
December 31, 2004	
December 31, 2004	

AP9–3.

Requirement 1

   2006: _____

_____

_____

   2007: _____

_____

_____

Requirement 2

_____

_____

_____

_____

_____

_____

_____

_____

_____

_____

Requirement 3

_____

_____

_____

_____

_____

_____

Requirement 4

_____

_____

_____

_____

_____

_____

Requirement 5

_____

_____

_____

_____

_____

_____

AP9–4.

a. _____

b. _____

c. _____

d. _____

e. _____

f. _____

g. _____

h. _____

i. _____

AP9–5. _____

_____
_____
_____
_____
_____
_____
_____
_____
_____
_____
_____
_____
_____
_____
_____
_____
_____
_____
_____
_____
_____
_____
_____

AP9–6.

Requirement 1

(a) Income tax payable: _____
      2006 _____
      2007 _____

(b) Deferred income tax: _____
   Expense: _____
      2006 _____
      2007 _____

   Revenue: _____
      2007 _____
      2008 _____

   Net deferred tax: _____
      2006 _____
      2007 _____
      2008 _____

Requirement 2

Entries to record income taxes:

	2006	2007
Income tax expense		
Deferred income tax liability		
Income tax payable		

Requirement 3

	2006	2007
Income Statement:		
Income tax expense		
Balance Sheet:		
Deferred income tax liability		
Income tax payable		

Name _____ Date _____ Course _____ Section_____

AP9–6. (continued)
Requirement 4

AP9–7.
Requirement 1

Requirement 2

Requirement 3

Requirement 4

AP9–8.

AP9–9.

Requirement 1

Requirement 2   **Fund Accumulation Schedule**

Date	Cash Payment	Interest Revenue	Fund Increase	Fund Balance
Totals				

Requirement 3

	December 31		
	2003	2004	2005
Plant addition fund			
Interest revenue			
Cash			

Requirement 4

January 1, 2006:	
Plant addition	
Plant addition fund	
Cash	

CP9–1.

Requirement 1
_____
_____
_____
_____

Requirement 2
_____
_____
_____
_____

Requirement 3
_____
_____
_____
_____

Requirement 4
_____
_____
_____
_____

Requirement 5
_____
_____
_____
_____

CP9–2.

Requirement 1
_____
_____
_____
_____

Requirement 2
_____
_____
_____
_____

Requirement 3
_____
_____
_____
_____

Requirement 4
_____
_____
_____
_____

Requirement 5
_____
_____
_____
_____

CP9–3.

Requirement 1

	American Eagle Outfitters	Abercrombie & Fitch
2000: Current Ratio		
1999: Current Ratio		

Requirement 2

	Industry Average	American Eagle Outfitters	Abercrombie & Fitch
Current Ratio =			

_____

_____

_____

_____

_____

_____

_____

_____

_____

_____

Requirement 3

	American Eagle Outfitters	Abercrombie & Fitch
2000: Accounts Payable Turnover Ratio		
1999: Accounts Payable Turnover Ratio		

Long-Term Liability

American Eagle _____

Abercrombie & Fitch _____

CP9–3. (continued)

Requirement 4

	Industry Average	American Eagle Outfitters	Abercrombie & Fitch
Payable Turnover =			

Requirement 5

CP9–4.

Requirement 1

Requirement 2

Name _____ Date _____ Course _____ Section _____

CP9–5.

_____

_____

_____

_____

_____

_____

_____

_____

_____

_____

_____

_____

_____

_____

_____

_____

_____

_____

_____

_____

_____

_____

_____

_____

CP9–6.

_____

_____

_____

_____

_____

_____

_____

_____

_____

_____

_____

_____

_____

_____

_____

_____

_____

_____

_____

_____

_____

_____

CP9–7.

Requirement 1

Requirement 2

CP9–8.

Present value computation:

Payment	PV Factor	Present Value

CP9–9.

	Current Ratio	Working Capital	Liquidity
a.			
b.			
c.			
d.			
e.			
f.			

CP9–10.

CP9–11.

CP9–12.

Requirement 1

_____

Requirement 2

_____

Requirement 3

_____

Requirement 4

_____

Requirement 5

_____

CP9–13.

_____
_____
_____
_____
_____
_____
_____
_____
_____
_____
_____
_____
_____

CP9–14.

_____
_____
_____
_____
_____
_____
_____
_____
_____
_____
_____
_____
_____
_____

CP9–15

M10–1.

1. _____
2. _____
3. _____
4. _____
5. _____
6. _____

M10–2.

M10–3.

M10–4.

M10–5.

M10–6.

M10–7.

M10–8.

M10–9.

E10–13.

Requirement 1

January 1, 2003:

Requirement 2

December 31, 2003:

Requirement 3

December 31, 2003:

Income Statement:

Balance Sheet:

E10–14.

Requirement 1

1. Issue price: _____

_____

_____

_____

_____

2. _____

_____

_____

_____

_____

3. Issuance entry:

Requirement 2

Coupon (stated interest) rate: _____

_____

_____

_____

_____

_____

_____

_____

_____

_____

Interest expense, December 31, 2003:

P10–4.

Requirement 1

Items	Case A	Case B	Case C
(a) Cash received at issue			
(b) Bond interest expense			
(c) Bonds payable			
(d) Unamortized discount			
(e) Unamortized premium			
(f) Net liability			
(g) Stated rate of interest			

P10–5.

Requirement 1

Requirement 2

Requirement 3

June 30, 2003:

December 31, 2003:

June 30, 2004:

Requirement 4

Income Statement for 2003:

Balance Sheet at December 31, 2003:

P10–6.

1.

Date	Cash	Interest	Amortization	Balance
Jan. 1, 2003				$ 6101
End of 2003	$ 450	$ 427	$ 23	6078
End of 2004	450			6053
End of 2005	450			
End of 2006	450			6000

Calculations: _____

_____

_____

_____

_____

_____

_____

_____

_____

_____

2. Maturity (par) amount: _____

_____

_____

_____

3. Cash received: _____

_____

_____

_____

4. Premium: _____

_____

_____

_____

5. Cash disbursed for interest: _____

_____

_____

_____

6. Effective-Interest amortization: _____

_____

_____

_____

P10–6. (concluded)

7. Stated interest rate:

_____

_____

_____

_____

8. Yield or effective rate of interest:

_____

_____

_____

_____

9. Interest expense:

_____

_____

_____

_____

10. Balance Sheet:

	2003	2004	2005	2006
Long-term liabilities:				

11. Evaluation of amortization methods:

_____

_____

_____

_____

_____

_____

_____

_____

_____

_____

_____

_____

_____

_____

_____

_____

_____

_____

P10–7.

Requirement 1

Requirement 2—Straight-line amortization:

	2003	2004	2005	2006	2007
(a) Cash interest payment	$	$	$	$	$
(b) Amortization of discount					
(c) Bond interest expense					

(d) Effective interest rate: _____

(e) Explanation of theoretical deficiency: _____

Requirement 3—Effective-interest amortization:

Bond Repayment Schedule

Date	Cash Payment	Interest Expense	Amortization of Discount	Net Liability

P10–7. (concluded)

Requirement 4

_____
_____
_____
_____
_____
_____
_____
_____
_____
_____
_____
_____
_____
_____
_____
_____
_____

P10–8.

Requirement 1

_____
_____
_____
_____

Requirement 2

_____
_____
_____
_____

AP10–1.

_____
_____
_____
_____
_____
_____
_____
_____
_____
_____
_____
_____
_____
_____

AP10–2.

Requirement 1

_____
_____
_____
_____
_____

Requirement 2

September 1, 2003

_____
_____
_____
_____
_____
_____
_____

Requirement 3

_____
_____
_____
_____
_____

Requirement 4

Date	Debt-to-Equity	Times-Interest-Earned
March 1, 2003		
September 1, 2003		
December 31, 2003		

AP10–3.

Requirement 1 (000's)

Items	At End of 2003	At End of 2004	At End of 2005	At End of 2006
Case A—Sold at par (100):				
Interest expense on income statement				
Net liability on balance sheet				
Case B—Sold at a discount (90):				
Interest expense on income statement				
Net liability on balance sheet				
Case C—Sold at a premium (110):				
Interest expense on income statement				
Net liability on balance sheet				

AP10–4.

Requirement 1

Requirement 2

Requirement 3

June 30, 2003:

December 31, 2003:

June 30, 2004:

Requirement 4

Income Statement for 2003:

Balance Sheet at December 31, 2003:

AP10–5.

Requirement 1—Bond issue price:

Requirement 2—Straight-line amortization:

	2003	2004	2005	2006	2007
(a) Cash interest payment	$	$	$	$	$
(b) Amortization of premium					
(c) Bond interest expense					

(d) Effective interest rate:

(e) Explanation of theoretical deficiency:

Name _____ Date _____ Course _____ Section_____

P10–5. (concluded)

Requirement 3—Effective-interest amortization:

Bond Repayment Schedule

Date	Cash Payment	Interest Expense	Amortization of Discount	Net Liability

Requirement 4

Name _____ Date _____ Course _____ Section _____

AP10–6.
Requirement 1

Requirement 2

Requirement 3

CP10–1.
Requirement 1

Requirement 2

Requirement 3

CP10–2.
Requirement 1

Requirement 2

Requirement 3

CP10–3.
Requirement 1

Requirement 2

CP10–4.

Requirement 1—Comparison of results:

Item	Actual Results for 2003								Increase in Debt of $80,000 and a Corresponding Decrease in Stockholders' Equity of $80,000							
(a) Total debt	$								$							
(b) Total assets																
(c) Total stockholders' equity																
(d) Interest expense (total 10%)																
(e) Net income																
(f) Return on total assets																
(g) Earnings available to stockholders:																
(1) Amount																
(2) Per share																
(3) Return on stockholders' equity																

Computations:

_____
_____
_____
_____
_____
_____
_____
_____
_____
_____
_____
_____
_____
_____
_____
_____
_____

Requirement 2—Interpretation:

_____
_____
_____
_____
_____
_____
_____
_____
_____
_____
_____
_____

CP10–5.

Requirement 1

_____

_____
_____
_____
_____
_____
_____
_____
_____
_____
_____
_____
_____
_____

Requirement 2

_____

_____
_____
_____
_____
_____

CP10–6.

1. _____

_____
_____
_____
_____

2. _____

_____
_____
_____
_____

3. _____

_____
_____
_____
_____
_____
_____
_____

CP10–7.

CP10–8.

CP10–9.

CP10–10.

CP10–11.

CP10–12.

CP10–13.

M11–1.

M11–2.

M11–3.

M11–4.

(blank ruled lines)

M11–5.

	Assets	Liabilities	Stockholders' Equity	Net Income
1.				
2.				
3.				

M11–6.

(blank ruled lines)

M11–7.

April 15, 2003:	

June 14, 2003:	

M11–8.

_____
_____
_____
_____
_____
_____
_____
_____
_____
_____
_____
_____

M11–9.

_____
_____
_____
_____
_____
_____
_____
_____
_____
_____
_____
_____
_____
_____
_____
_____
_____

M11–10.

E11–1.

Requirement 1

Requirement 2

Stockholders' Equity

Contributed capital:											
Total contributed capital											
Retained earnings											
Total Stockholders' Equity											

Requirement 3

E11–2.

Requirement 1

Requirement 2

E11–3.

Stockholders' Equity

Contributed capital:							
Retained earnings							
Total Stockholders' Equity							

E11–4.

Requirement 1

Stockholders' Equity

Contributed capital:							

Requirement 2

E11–5.

Requirement 1

Requirement 2

E11–6.

Requirement 1
Shares issued (preferred):
_____
_____
_____

Requirement 2
Shares outstanding (preferred):
_____
_____
_____

Requirement 3
Average sales price per share (preferred):
_____
_____
_____

Requirement 4
Decrease in corporate resources:
_____
_____
_____

Requirement 5
Decrease in stockholders' equity from treasury stock:
_____
_____
_____

Requirement 6
Treasury stock—cost per share:
_____
_____
_____

Requirement 7
Total stockholders' equity:
_____
_____
_____

Requirement 8
Average issue price (common):
_____
_____
_____
_____

Requirement 9
Cost of treasury stock (balance):
_____
_____
_____
_____

E11–7.

Requirement 1

_____

_____
_____
_____
_____
_____
_____
_____
_____
_____
_____
_____

Requirement 2

_____
_____
_____
_____
_____
_____
_____
_____
_____
_____
_____
_____
_____
_____

Requirement 3

_____
_____
_____
_____
_____
_____
_____
_____
_____

E11–8.

Requirement 1

February 1, 2005:																

July 15, 2005:

September 1, 2005:

December 15, 2005:

Requirement 2

Requirement 3

E11–9.

Computation of treasury stock:

Computation of shares outstanding:

E11–10.

Requirement 1

	Preferred (_____ Shares)	Common (_____ Shares)	Total
(a) Noncumulative:			
Preferred			
Balance to common			
Per share			
(b) Cumulative:			

	a	b

Requirement 2

Requirement 3

E11–11.

_____
_____
_____
_____
_____
_____
_____
_____
_____
_____
_____
_____
_____
_____
_____
_____
_____
_____
_____
_____
_____
_____
_____
_____
_____
_____

E11–12.

Item	Effect of Cash Dividend (Preferred)	Effect of Stock Dividend (Common)
Assets		
Liabilities		
Stockholders' equity		

E11–13.

Computation of shares outstanding:

E11–14.
Requirement 1

	Stockholders' Equity	
	Before Stock Dividends	After Stock Dividends
Contributed Capital:		
Common Stock		
Retained earnings		
Total stockholders' equity		

Computations:

E11–14. (continued)
Requirement 2

Item	Effects of Stock Dividend
Assets	
Liabilities	
Stockholders' equity	

E11–15.
Requirement 1

_____
_____
_____
_____
_____
_____
_____

Requirement 2

_____
_____
_____
_____
_____
_____
_____

Requirement 3

_____
_____
_____
_____
_____
_____
_____

E11–16.

Requirement 1

Stockholders' Equity—December 31, 2007

Contributed capital:									

Requirement 2

E11–17.

E11–18.

Comparative results:

Item	Before Dividend and Split	After Stock Dividend	After Stock Split
Common stock account			
Par per share			
Shares outstanding			
Contributed capital in excess of par			
Retained earnings			
Total stockholders' equity			

Comments: _____

_____

_____

_____

_____

_____

_____

_____

_____

_____

_____

_____

_____

_____

E11–19.

Requirement 1 _____

_____

_____

_____

_____

Requirement 2 _____

_____

_____

_____

_____

_____

_____

_____

_____

_____

_____

E11–20.

Requirement 1

_____
_____
_____
_____
_____
_____
_____
_____
_____
_____

Requirement 2

_____
_____
_____
_____
_____
_____

P11–1.

1.

2.

3.

4.

5.

6.

7.

8.

P11–2.

Stockholders' Equity—December 31, 2003

Contributed capital:										

P11–3.

Requirement 1

(a)

(b)

(c)

Requirement 2

P11–4.

Requirement 1

Requirement 2

Requirement 3

Requirement 4

P11–5.

Stockholders' Equity—December 31, 2003

Contributed capital:															

P11–6.

(a)

(b)

(c)

P11–7.

Requirement 1

_____
_____
_____
_____
_____
_____
_____
_____
_____

Requirement 2

_____
_____
_____
_____
_____
_____
_____
_____
_____

Requirement 3

_____
_____
_____
_____
_____
_____
_____
_____
_____

Requirement 4

_____
_____
_____
_____
_____
_____
_____
_____
_____

P11–8.

Requirement 1

	Preferred (6,000 Shares)	Common (30,000 Shares)	Total
Case A—Preferred is noncumulative:			
Case B—Preferred is cumulative:			
Case C—Preferred is cumulative:			

Requirement 2

P11–8. (concluded)

Requirement 2 (continued)

Schedule of Comparative Differences (with comments)

Item	Amount of Dollar Increase (Decrease)	
	Cash Dividend—Case C	Stock Dividend
Assets		
Liabilities		
Stockholders' equity		

Comments: _____

_____
_____
_____
_____
_____
_____
_____
_____
_____
_____
_____

P11–9.

Requirement 1

_____

Requirement 2

_____

P11–10.

Item	Comparative Effects Explained	
	Cash Dividend on Preferred	Stock Dividend on Common
(a) Through December 31, 2004:		
Assets		
Liabilities		
Stockholders' equity		

(b) On February 15, 2005:

Item	Cash Dividend on Preferred	Stock Dividend on Common
Assets		
Liabilities		
Stockholders' equity		

(c) Overall Effects from December 1, 2004, through February 15, 2005:

Item	Cash Dividend on Preferred	Stock Dividend on Common
Assets		
Liabilities		
Stockholders' equity		

P11–11.

Requirement 1

Requirement 2

Requirement 3

P11–12.

Requirement 1

Case A: Sole Proprietorship, closing entries:

Case B: Partnership, closing entries:

Case C: Corporation, closing entries:

Requirement 2

Case A: Sole Proprietorship:

Statement of Owner's Equity

P11–12. (concluded)

Case B: Partnership:

Partners' Equity

Statement of Partners' Equity

	A	B	Total
Partners' equity, January 1, 2003			

Case C: Corporation:

Stockholders' Equity

Contributed capital:	

Statement of Retained Earnings

Retained earnings, balance January 1, 2003	

AP11–1.

Requirement 1

_____

_____

_____

_____

_____

_____

_____

_____

_____

Requirement 2

_____

_____

Requirement 3

_____

_____

Requirement 4

_____

_____

Requirement 5

_____

_____

Requirement 6

_____

_____

_____

_____

Requirement 7

_____

_____

_____

AP11–2.

Requirement 1

Requirement 2

AP11–3.

Requirement 1   Stockholders' Equity—December 31, 2003

Contributed capital:												

AP11–4.

(a)																
(b)																
(c)																
(d)																

AP11–5.

Requirement 1

	Preferred	Common	Total
Case A—Preferred is noncumulative:			
Case B—Preferred is cumulative:			
Case C—Preferred is cumulative:			

Requirement 2

Schedule of Comparative Differences (with comments)

Item	Amount of Dollar Increase (Decrease)	
	Cash Dividend—Case C	Stock Dividend
Assets		
Liabilities		
Stockholders' equity		

Comments:

CP11–1.

Requirement 1

_____

_____

Requirement 2

_____

_____

Requirement 3

_____

_____

Requirement 4

_____

_____

Requirement 5

_____

_____

Requirement 6

_____

_____

CP11–2.

Requirement 1

_____

_____

_____

Requirement 2

_____

_____

Requirement 3

_____

_____

_____

Requirement 4

_____

_____

_____

Requirement 5

_____

_____

_____

_____

Requirement 6

_____

_____

_____

CP11–3.
Requirement 1

Requirement 2

Requirement 3

Requirement 4

CP11–4.

CP11–5.

CP11–6.

CP11–7.

CP11–8.

CP11–9.

CP11–10.

CP11–11.

CP11–12.

CP11–13.

M12–1.

_____ More than 50 percent ownership.

_____ Bonds held to maturity.

_____ Less than 20 percent ownership.

_____ Current market value.

_____ Original cost less any amortization of premium or discount associated with the purchase.

_____ Original cost plus part of the income of the investee less proportionate part of the dividends declared by the investee.

M12–2.

M12–3.

July 2, 2004:

December 15, 2004:

December 31, 2004:

M12–4.

July 2, 2004:

December 15, 2004:

December 31, 2004:

M12–5.

Transaction	Balance Sheet			Income Statement		
	Assets	Liabilities	Stockholders' Equity	Revenues	Expenses	Net Income

M12–6.

Transaction	Balance Sheet			Income Statement		
	Assets	Liabilities	Stockholders' Equity	Revenues	Expenses	Net Income

M12–7.

July 2, 2003:

December 31, 2003:

M12–8.

	Balance Sheet			Income Statement		
Transaction	Asset	Liabilities	Stockholders' Equity	Revenues	Expenses	Net Income

M12–9.

M12–10.

	2004	2005	2006
Net income / Average total assets	= _____	_____	_____
Return on assets	= _____	_____	_____

M12–11.

E12–1.

E12–2.

Question	Method of Measurement	
	Market Value Method	Equity Method
a.		
b.		
c.		
d.		
e.		
f.		
g.		

E12–3.

June 30, 2003:				
December 31, 2003:				
December 31, 2004:				
December 31, 2005:				

Computations:

Year	Market	–	Cost	=	Allowance Balance	–	Unadjusted Balance	=	Adjustment
2003									
2004									
2005									

Feb. 14, 2006:				

E12–4.

June 30, 2003:														
December 31, 2003:														
December 31, 2004:														
December 31, 2005:														

Computations:

Year	Market	–	Cost	=	Allowance Balance	–	Unadjusted Balance	=	Adjustment
2003									
2004									
2005									

Feb. 14, 2006:								

E12–5.

March 10, 2004:		
Dec. 31, 2004:		
Dec. 31, 2005:		
Dec. 31, 2006:		

Computations:

Year	Market	–	Cost	=	Allowance Balance	–	Unadjusted Balance	=	Adjustment
2004									
2005									
2006									

Sept. 12, 2007:		

E12–6.

March 10, 2004:						
Dec. 31, 2004:						
Dec. 31, 2005:						
Dec. 31, 2006:						

Computations:

Year	Market	–	Cost	=	Allowance Balance	–	Unadjusted Balance	=	Adjustment
2004									
2005									
2006									

Sept. 12, 2007:						

E12–7.

Requirement 1

Requirement 2

January 10, 2004:

December 31, 2004:

December 31, 2004:

Requirement 3

Balance Sheet—At December 31, 2004

Income Statement —For the Year Ended December 31, 2004

E12–8.

1. _____

_____

_____

_____

2. _____

_____

_____

_____

E12–9.

E12–10.

1.

$$\text{Return on assets} \quad = \quad \frac{\text{Net income}}{\text{Average total assets}} \quad =$$

2. _____

_____

_____

_____

_____

E12–11.

_____

_____

_____

_____

_____

_____

_____

_____

_____

_____

Name _____ Date _____ Course _____ Section _____

E12–12.

Requirement 1

Requirement 2

Requirement 3

COMPANY P AND ITS SUBSIDIARY, COMPANY S (100% OWNED)
Consolidated Balance Sheet (purchase method)
January 1, 2003 (immediately after acquisition)

| | Separate Balance Sheets | | Eliminations | Consolidated Balance Sheet |
	Company P	Company S		

E12–11.

Goodwill calculation:							
Revenues							
Expenses							
Net Income							

P12–1.

Requirement 1

Requirement 2

Requirement 3

P12–2.

Requirement 1

March 1, 2003:
Dec. 31, 2003:
Dec. 31, 2004:
Dec. 31, 2005:

Requirement 2

March 1, 2003:
Dec. 31, 2003:
Dec. 31, 2004:
Dec. 31, 2005:

Computations:

Year	Market	–	Cost	=	Allowance Balance	–	Unadjusted Balance	=	Adjustment
2003									
2004									
2005									

P12–3.

Requirement 1

_____
_____
_____
_____
_____
_____
_____
_____
_____
_____

Requirement 2

a.

	2004	2005

Q common stock:	=	
R preferred stock:	=	
Total investment		

b.

_____
_____
_____
_____
_____

c. Dividends received:

	2004	2005

2004:	Q common stock:	=	
	R preferred stock:	=	
	Total		
2005:	Q Common stock:	=	
	R preferred stock:	=	
	Total		

P12–3. (continued)

d.

	2004	2005
Market value effects:		
Net unrealized gain/loss – SAS (SE)		
Valuation allowance – SAS (A)		
Valuation allowance – SAS (A)		
Net unrealized gain/loss –SAS (SE)		

Computations:

Year	Market	–	Cost	=	Allowance Balance	–	Unadjusted Balance	=	Adjustment
2004: Q									
2004: R									
2005: Q									
2005: R									

Requirement 3

	2004	2005
a.		
b.		
c.		

P12–4.
Requirement 1

Aug. 4, 2002:			
Dec. 31, 2002:			
June 1, 2003:			
Dec. 31, 2003:			
June 1, 2004:			
Dec. 31, 2004:			

Computations:

Year	Market	–	Cost	=	Allowance Balance	–	Unadjusted Balance	=	Adjustment
2002									
2003									
2004									

P12–4. (continued)

Requirement 2

Aug. 4, 2002:																					
Dec. 31, 2002:																					
June 1, 2003:																					
Dec. 31, 2003:																					
June 1, 2004:																					
Dec. 31, 2004:																					

Requirement 3

Aug. 4, 2002:																					
Dec. 31, 2002:																					
June 1, 2003:																					
Dec. 31, 2003:																					
June 1, 2004:																					
Dec. 31, 2004:																					

P12–5.

Requirement 1

Case A: _____
_____
_____
_____
_____
_____
_____

Case B: _____
_____
_____
_____
_____
_____
_____
_____

Requirement 2

		Case A—12%	Case B—35%
a.			
b.			
c.			
d.			

P12–5. (concluded)

Requirement 3

Balance Sheet:	Case A—12%	Case B—35%
Income Statement:		

Requirement 4

P12–6.

Requirement 1

Case A: _____
_____
_____
_____
_____
_____

Case B: _____
_____
_____
_____
_____
_____
_____

Requirement 2

		Case A—10%	Case B—40%
a.			
b.			
c.			
d.			

P12–6. (concluded)

Requirement 3

Balance Sheet:	Case A	Case B
Income Statement:		

Requirement 4

_____

_____

_____

_____

_____

_____

P12–7.

_____

_____

_____

_____

_____

_____

_____

_____

_____

_____

_____

_____

_____

_____

_____

_____

_____

_____

_____

P12–8.

Requirement 1

Requirement 2

Requirement 3

PRONTI COMPANY
Consolidated Balance Sheet
January 4, 2004 (immediately after acquisition)

P12–9.

Requirement 1

	2000	1999	1998
$\dfrac{\text{Net income}}{\text{Average total assets}}$ =	_____	_____	_____
Return on assets =	_____	_____	_____

_____
_____
_____
_____
_____
_____
_____
_____

Requirement 2

_____
_____
_____
_____
_____
_____
_____
_____
_____
_____

P12–10.

Requirement 1

Requirement 2

Requirement 3

Requirement 4

PENN COMPANY AND SUBSIDIARY
Consolidated Balance Sheet
January 4, 2004 (immediately after acquisition)

	Separate Balance Sheets		Eliminations	Consolidated Balance Sheet
	Company P	Company S		

AP12–1.

Requirement 1

_____
_____
_____
_____
_____
_____
_____
_____
_____
_____

Requirement 2

_____
_____
_____
_____
_____
_____
_____
_____
_____
_____

Requirement 3

_____
_____
_____
_____
_____
_____
_____
_____
_____
_____

AP12–2.

Requirement 1

Sept. 15, 2004:									
Dec. 31, 2004:									
Dec. 31, 2005:									
Dec. 31, 2006:									

Computations:

Year	Market	–	Cost	=	Allowance Balance	–	Unadjusted Balance	=	Adjustment
2004									
2005									
2006									

Requirement 2

Sept. 15, 2004:								
Dec. 31, 2004:								
Dec. 31, 2005:								
Dec. 31, 2006:								

AP12–3.

Requirement 1

Requirement 2

a.

	2003	2004

b.

	2003	2004
c.		
d.		

Requirement 3

	2003	2004
a.		
b.		
c.		

AP12–4.

Requirement 1

Case A: _____

_____

_____

_____

_____

_____

_____

Case B: _____

_____

_____

_____

_____

_____

_____

_____

_____

Requirement 2

	Case A—15%	Case B—40%

AP12–4. (continued)

Requirement 3

December 31, 2005:	Case A	Case B
Balance sheet (partial):		

AP12–5.

	Case A	Case B

AP12–6.

Requirement 1

Requirement 2

Requirement 3

Pi COMPANY
Consolidated Balance Sheet
June 1, 2003 (immediately after acquisition)

AP12–7.

Requirement 1 2000 1999 1998

$$\frac{\text{Net income}}{\text{Average total assets}} =$$ _____ _____ _____

Return on assets = _____ _____ _____

_____

_____

_____

_____

_____

_____

_____

_____

Requirement 2

_____

_____

_____

_____

_____

_____

_____

_____

_____

_____

_____

CP12–1.

1. _____

_____

_____

_____

_____

_____

_____

_____

2. _____

_____

_____

_____

_____

_____

_____

_____

_____

3. _____

_____

_____

_____

_____

_____

_____

_____

4. _____

_____

_____

_____

5. _____

_____

_____

_____

_____

_____

CP12–2.

1. _____

_____
_____

2. _____

_____
_____
_____
_____
_____
_____
_____
_____

3.

ROA Analysis	2000	1999
Net Income/Average Total Assets		

CP12–3.

1.

ROA Analysis	American Eagle Outfitters	Abercrombie & Fitch
$\dfrac{\text{Net Income}}{\text{Net Sales}}$		
$\dfrac{\text{Net Sales}}{\text{Average Total Assets}}$		
Return on Assets		

2. _____

_____
_____
_____
_____
_____

3. _____

_____
_____
_____

CP12–4.
Requirement 1

Requirement 2

Requirement 3

Requirement 4

518

CP12–5.

Requirement 1

Requirement 2

Requirement 3

CP12–6.

CP12–7.

CP12–8.

CP12–9.

E13–7.
Requirement 1
Cash flows from operating activities—indirect method

Requirement 2

E13–8.
Requirement 1
Cash flows from operating activities—indirect method

Requirement 2

E13–9.

Account	Change
Receivables	
Inventories	
Other current assets	
Payables	

E13–10.

Account	Change
Accounts receivables	
Inventories	
Other current assets	
Accounts payables	
Income taxes payable	
Other current liabilities	

E13–11.

Requirement 1

Cash flows from operating activities—direct method

Requirement 2

E13–16.

Requirement 1

$$\text{Capital acquisitions ratio} = \frac{\text{Cash flow from operations}}{\text{Cash Paid for Plant \& Equipment}} = \underline{\hspace{2cm}} = \underline{\hspace{2cm}}$$

Requirement 2

_____
_____
_____
_____
_____
_____
_____

Requirement 3

_____
_____
_____
_____

E13–17.

Requirement 1

_____
_____
_____
_____
_____
_____
_____
_____
_____
_____
_____
_____
_____
_____

Requirement 2

_____
_____
_____
_____
_____
_____
_____
_____
_____
_____

E13–18.

	1993	1992	1991

E13–19.

Equipment		Accumulated Depreciation	

Computations:

E13–20.

Item	Balances 12/31/2003	Analysis		Balances 12/31/2004
		Debit	Credit	
Cash plus short-term investments				
Noncash accounts:				
Accounts receivable (net)				
Merchandise inventory				
Investments, long-term				
Operational assets				
Total				
Accumulated depreciation				
Accounts payable				
Wages payable				
Income taxes payable				
Bonds payable				
Common stock, no par				
Retained earnings				
Total				

		Inflows	Outflows	
Statement of Cash Inflows (Outflows)				
Conversion of net income to cash flow from				
operating activities:				

P13–1.

FRANK CORPORATION
Statement of Cash Flows
For the Year Ended December 31, 2004

Cash flows from operating activities:					
Cash flows from investing activities:					
Cash flows from financing activities:					

P13–2.

ROCKY MOUNTAIN CHOCOLATE FACTORY, INC.
Statement of Cash Flows
For the Quarter Ended May 31, 1996

Cash flows from operating activities:			
Cash flows from investing activities:			
Cash flows from financing activities:			

P13–3.

FRANK CORPORATION
Statement of Cash Flows
For the Year Ended December 31, 2004

Cash flows from operating activities:											
Cash flows from investing activities:											
Cash flows from financing activities:											

P13–4.

Requirement 1

BETA COMPANY
Cash Flows from Operating Activities
Direct Method

Cash flows from operating activities:						

Requirement 2

BETA COMPANY
Cash Flows from Operating Activities
Indirect Method

Cash flows from operating activities:									

P13–5.

Requirement 1

HUNTER COMPANY
Statement of Cash Flows Spreadsheet
For the Year Ended December 31, 2004

	12/31/2003	Debit	Ref.	Credit	Ref.	12/31/2004
BALANCE SHEET						

	Inflow	Ref.	Outflow	Ref.	
STATEMENT OF CASH FLOWS— INDIRECT METHOD					

P13–5. (continued)

Requirement 2

HUNTER COMPANY
Statement of Cash Flows
For the Year Ended December 31, 2004

Cash flows from operating activities:							
Cash flows from investing activities:							
Cash flows from financing activities:							

Requirement 3

AP13–1.

STONEWALL COMPANY
Statement of Cash Flows
For the Year Ended December 31, 2003

Cash flows from operating activities:														
Cash flows from investing activities:														
Cash flows from financing activities:														

AP13–2.

Requirement 1

ELLINGTON COMPANY
Statement of Cash Flows Spreadsheet
For the Year Ended December 31, 2004

	12/31/2003	Debit	Ref.	Credit	Ref.	12/31/2004
BALANCE SHEET						

(continued)

AP13–2. (continued)

Requirement 1 (continued)

	Inflow	Ref.	Outflow	Ref.	
STATEMENT OF CASH FLOWS—INDIRECT METHOD					

AP13–2. (concluded)

Requirement 2

ELLINGTON COMPANY
Statement of Cash Flows
For the Year Ended December 31, 2004

Requirement 3

Schedule of Noncash
Investing and Financing Activities

CP13–1.

1. _____
_____
_____

2. _____
_____
_____
_____

3. _____
_____
_____
_____
_____
_____
_____
_____
_____
_____

4. _____
_____
_____
_____
_____
_____
_____
_____
_____
_____
_____
_____
_____

5. _____
_____
_____
_____
_____
_____
_____
_____
_____
_____
_____

CP13–2.

1. _____

_____

_____

_____

_____

_____

_____

_____

_____

_____

_____

_____

_____

_____

_____

2. _____

_____

_____

_____

_____

_____

_____

_____

_____

_____

_____

_____

_____

_____

_____

_____

_____

_____

_____

3. _____

_____

_____

_____

_____

_____

_____

_____

_____

_____

_____

_____

CP13–3.

1.

	Abercrombie & Fitch	American Eagle Outfitters
Quality of income ratio $=$ $\dfrac{\text{Cash flow from operations}}{\text{Net income}}$	_____ =	_____ =

2.

	Industry Average	Abercrombie & Fitch	American Eagle Outfitters
Quality of Income =			

	Industry Average	Abercrombie & Fitch	American Eagle Outfitters
Sales Growth =			

CP13–3. (continued)

3.

	Abercrombie & Fitch	American Eagle Outfitters
Capital acquisitions ratio $=$ $\dfrac{\text{Cash flow from operations}}{\text{Cash Paid for Plant \& Equipment}}$	_____ =	_____ =

_____
_____
_____
_____
_____
_____
_____
_____
_____

4.

	Industry Average	Abercrombie & Fitch	American Eagle Outfitters
Capital Acquisitions $=$			

_____
_____
_____
_____
_____
_____

Name _____ Date _____ Course _____ Section _____

CP13–4.

1.

2.

548

CP13–5.

CP13–6.

M14–1.

M14–2.

M14–3.

M14–4.

M14–5.

M14–6.

_____
_____
_____
_____
_____
_____
_____
_____
_____
_____

M14–7.

_____
_____
_____
_____
_____
_____
_____
_____
_____
_____
_____

M14–8.

_____
_____
_____
_____
_____
_____
_____
_____
_____
_____
_____

M14–9.

_____
_____
_____
_____
_____
_____
_____
_____
_____
_____

M14–10.

_____
_____
_____
_____
_____
_____
_____
_____
_____
_____
_____
_____
_____
_____

E14–1.

_____ 1. Profit margin
_____ 2. Inventory turnover ratio
_____ 3. Average collection period
_____ 4. Creditors' equity to total equities
_____ 5. Dividend yield ratio
_____ 6. Return on equity
_____ 7. Current ratio
_____ 8. Debt/equity ratio
_____ 9. Price/earnings ratio
_____ 10. Financial leverage percentage

_____ 11. Receivable turnover ratio
_____ 12. Average days' supply of inventory
_____ 13. Owners' equity to total equities
_____ 14. Earnings per share
_____ 15. Return on assets
_____ 16. Quick ratio
_____ 17. Times interest earned
_____ 18. Cash coverage ratio
_____ 19. Fixed asset turnover

E14–2.

	2000	1999
Cost of Sales		
Selling		
Interest Expense		
Interest Income		
Income Tax Expense		
Other Income		
Net Earnings		

_____
_____
_____
_____
_____

E14–3.

	Current Assets		Current Liabilities		Working Capital	Current Ratio
Start						
Transaction (1)						
Transaction (2)						

E14–4.

_____
_____
_____
_____
_____
_____
_____
_____
_____
_____
_____

E14–5.

Turnover:

_____
_____
_____
_____

Days:

_____
_____
_____
_____

E14–6.

	%

E14–7.

	Current Assets		Current Liabilities		Working Capital	Current Ratio
Start						
Transaction (1)						
Transaction (2)						
Transaction (3)						
Transaction (4)						

E14–8.

_____
_____
_____
_____
_____
_____
_____
_____
_____
_____
_____
_____
_____
_____
_____
_____
_____
_____
_____

E14–9.

Turnover:

Days:

E14–10.

	Current Assets	Current Liabilities	Working Capital	Current Ratio
Start				
Transaction (1)				
Transaction (2)				
Transaction (3)				
Transaction (4)				
Transaction (5)				
Transaction (6)				

E14–11.

_____
_____
_____
_____
_____
_____
_____
_____
_____
_____
_____
_____
_____
_____
_____
_____
_____
_____
_____
_____
_____
_____
_____
_____
_____

E14–12.

1. _____

2. _____

3. _____

4. _____
_____

E14–13.

1. _____

2. _____

3. _____

4. _____
_____
_____

E14–14.

1. _____

_____

2. _____

_____

3. _____

_____

4. _____

_____

_____

_____

E14–15

1. _____

_____

2. _____

_____

3. _____

_____

4. _____

_____

_____

_____

P14–1.

Requirement 1

	Increase (Decrease) 2004 over 2003	
	Amount	Percent
Income Statement:		%
Balance Sheet:		

Requirement 2
Working capital:

	2004	2003

Change: _____

_____

_____

_____

_____

_____

_____

P14–2. (Based on data given in Problem 14-1)

Requirement 1

	Component Percentages 2004
Income Statement:	%
Balance Sheet:	

P14–2. (continued)
Requirement 2

a. Average percentage markup on sales	%
b. Average income tax rate	%
c. Profit margin	%
d. Investment in operational assets	%
e. Debt/equity ratio	%
f. Return on owners' investment	%
g. Return on assets	%
h. Financial leverage percentage	%

P14–3.
(Based on data given in Problem 14-1)

Name and Computation of the Ratio	Brief Explanation of the Ratio
Tests of profitability:	
(1)	
(2)	
(3)	
(4)	
(5)	
(6)	
(7)	

P14–3. (continued)

Name and Computation of the Ratio	Brief Explanation of the Ratio
Tests of liquidity:	
(1)	
(2)	
(3)	
(4)	
(5)	

P14–3. (continued)

Name and Computation of the Ratio	Brief Explanation of the Ratio
Tests of solvency and equity position:	
(1)	
(2)	
(3)	
(4)	
(5)	
Market tests:	
(1)	
(2)	

P14–4.

P14–5.

Requirement 1

Name and Computation of the Ratio	Brief Explanation of the Ratio
Tests of profitability:	
(1)	
(2)	
(3)	
(4)	
(5)	
(6)	

P14–5. (continued)

Requirement 1 (continued)

Name and Computation of the Ratio	Brief Explanation of the Ratio
Tests of liquidity:	
(1)	
(2)	
(3)	
(4)	
(5)	

P14–5. (continued)

Requirement 1 (concluded)

Name and Computation of the Ratio	Brief Explanation of the Ratio
Tests of solvency and equity position:	
(1)	
(2)	
(3)	
(4)	
Market tests:	
(1)	
(2)	

P14–5. (concluded)

Requirement 2

P14–6.

P14–7.

Requirement 1

Ratio	Armstrong Company	Blair Company
Test of Profitability:		
1. Return on equity		
2. Return on assets		
3. Financial leverage percentage		
4. Earnings per share		
5. Profit margin		
6. Fixed asset turnover		
Test of liquidity:		
7. Cash ratio		
8. Current ratio		
9. Quick ratio		
10. Receivable turnover		
11. Inventory turnover		
Solvency and equity position:		
12. Debt/equity ratio		
13. Owners' equity to total equities		
14. Creditors' equity to total equities		
Market tests:		
15. Price/earnings ratio		
16. Dividend yield ratio		

P14–7. (concluded)

Requirement 2

P14–8.

P14–9.

Ratio	Computation
Return on equity	
Return on assets	
Financial leverage percentage	
Earnings per share	
Quality of Income	
Profit Margin	
Fixed asset turnover	
Cash ratio	
Current ratio	

P14–9. (continued)

Ratio	Computation
Quick ratio	
Receivable turnover	
Inventory turnover	
Times interest earned	
Cash coverage	
Debt/Equity	
Price earnings	
Dividend Yield	

P14–10.

P14–11.

AP14–1.

Requirement 1

a.   *Tests of profitability:*

   (1) _____
   _____

   (2) _____
   _____

   (3) _____
   _____

   (4) _____
   _____

   (5) _____
   _____
   _____

b.   *Tests of liquidity:*

   (6) _____
   _____

   (7) _____
   _____

   (8) _____
   _____
   _____

   (9) _____
   _____
   _____
   _____

c.   *Tests of solvency:*

   (10) _____
   _____

   (11) _____
   _____

   (12) _____
   _____
   _____

d.   *Market tests:*

   (13) _____
   _____

   (14) _____
   _____
   _____
   _____
   _____
   _____

AP14–1. (concluded)

Requirement 2

		%
a. Sales revenue		
Income before extraordinary items		
Net income		
Cash		
Inventory		
Debt		
b. Pretax interest rate on long-term note:		

Requirement 3

Potential problems: _____

_____

_____

_____

_____

_____

_____

_____

_____

_____

_____

_____

_____

_____

_____

_____

_____

_____

AP14–2.

Requirement 1

Ratio	2003	2004	2005	2006
a. Profit margin %				
b. Gross margin ratio				
c. Expenses as a percentage of sales excluding cost of goods sold				
d. Inventory turnover				
e. Days' supply in inventory				
f. Receivable turnover				
g. Average days to collect				

Computations:

AP14–2. (concluded)

Requirement 2

Requirement 3

AP14–3.

AP14–4.

Requirement 1

Ratio	Rand Company	Tand Company
Test of Profitability:		
1. Return on equity		
2. Return on assets		
3. Financial leverage percentage		
4. Earnings per share		
5. Profit margin		
6. Fixed asset turnover		
Test of liquidity:		
7. Cash ratio		
8. Current ratio		
9. Quick ratio		
10. Receivable turnover		
11. Inventory turnover		
Solvency and equity position:		
12. Debt/equity ratio		
13. Owners' equity to total equities		
14. Creditors' equity to total equities		
Market tests:		
15. Price/earnings ratio		
16. Dividend yield ratio		

AP14–4. (concluded)

Requirement 2

AP14–5.

Ratio	Computation
Return on equity	
Return on assets	
Financial leverage percentage	
Earnings per share	
Quality of Income	
Profit Margin	
Fixed asset turnover	
Cash ratio	
Current ratio	

AP14–5. (continued)

Ratio	Computation
Quick ratio	
Receivable turnover	
Inventory turnover	
Times interest earned	
Cash coverage	
Debt/Equity	
Price earnings	
Dividend Yield	

AP14–6.

AP14–7.

CP14–1.

AMERICAN EAGLE

Ratio	Computation
Return on equity	
Return on assets	
Financial leverage percentage	
Earnings per share	
Quality of Income	
Profit Margin	
Fixed asset turnover	
Cash ratio	
Current ratio	

Name _____ Date _____ Course _____ Section _____

CP14–1. (continued)

Ratio	Computation
Quick ratio	
Receivable turnover	
Inventory turnover	
Times interest earned	
Cash coverage	
Debt/Equity	
Price earnings	
Dividend Yield	

CP14–2.

ABERCROMBIE & FITCH

Ratio	Computation
Return on equity	
Return on assets	
Financial leverage percentage	
Earnings per share	
Quality of Income	
Profit Margin	
Fixed asset turnover	
Cash ratio	
Current ratio	

CP14–2. (continued)

Ratio	Computation
Quick ratio	
Receivable turnover	
Inventory turnover	
Times interest earned	
Cash coverage	
Debt/Equity	
Price earnings	
Dividend Yield	

CP14–3.

	American Eagle	Abercrombie & Fitch	Industry Average
Return on equity			
Return on assets			
Financial leverage percentage			
Quality of income			
Net profit margin			
Fixed asset turnover			
Current ratio			
Quick ratio			
Inventory turnover			
Debt/Equity			
Price earnings			
Dividend yield			

Name _____ Date _____ Course _____ Section _____

CP14–4.
Case 1
_____
_____
_____
_____
_____
_____
_____
_____
_____
_____
_____
_____
_____
_____

Case 2
_____
_____
_____
_____
_____
_____
_____
_____
_____
_____
_____
_____
_____
_____
_____

Case 3
_____
_____
_____
_____
_____
_____
_____
_____
_____
_____
_____
_____
_____
_____
_____
_____
_____
_____

CP14–4. (continued)
Case 4

CP14–5.

CP14–6.

CP14–7.

_____
_____
_____
_____
_____
_____
_____
_____
_____
_____
_____

CP14–8.

Requirement 1

_____
_____
_____
_____
_____
_____
_____
_____
_____
_____
_____
_____
_____
_____
_____
_____
_____

Requirement 2

_____
_____
_____
_____
_____
_____
_____
_____
_____
_____
_____
_____
_____
_____

CP14–9.

Transaction	Current Ratio	Quick Ratio	Working Capital
a.			
b.			
c.			
d.			
e.			

CP14–10.

_____
_____
_____
_____
_____
_____
_____
_____
_____
_____
_____
_____
_____
_____
_____

CP14–11.

_____
_____
_____
_____
_____
_____
_____
_____
_____
_____
_____
_____
_____
_____
_____